Praise for *Way of the Doctor*

Love *Doctor Who*? Want t(
Then let Courtland Lewis
it means to be a good per
from Gallifrey.

Massimo Pigliucci, K.D. .... ol Philosophy at the City College of New York. Author of several books, including his most recent, *How to be a Stoic: Using Ancient Philosophy to Live a Modern Life*.

Grab your bow-tie (because bow-ties are cool) and don your fez, it's time to learn to be a *flâneur*—someone who is intimately engaged with others and his/her surroundings in order to gain a genuine understanding of the people and culture in one's life, like the Doctor. In *Way of the Doctor*, Lewis takes us on an entertaining and enlightening journey into the examined life of the Doctor, getting us "into the thick of things" with the moral dilemmas faced by the Doctor, the mission to avoid the "monsters" who threaten us with their evil actions, the quest for wisdom and knowledge, and, importantly, how to deal with endings. In short, this is a guidebook showing us how to "lead a better life" with the Doctor as our exemplar. As the Doctor says, "You've got to throw yourself in!" so embrace your inner *flâneur* and engage with *life*. Geronimo!

Paula Smithka, Associate Professor of Philosophy at the University of Southern Mississippi. Co-editor of Doctor Who and Philosophy, More Doctor Who and Philosophy, and Community, Diversity, and Difference: Implications for Peace.

Courtland Lewis' *Way of the Doctor* is a fantastic journey through some of life's most important questions. *Way of the Doctor* helps us discover the Doctor's lessons on how to think, how to live, what it means to know, what's right, what's wrong, what's good, what's evil, and even what it means to truly be human. Fans of *Doctor Who* won't be too surprised to learn that some of the most profound lessons about human flourishing have been taught to us by a Gallifreyan with a sonic screwdriver. While he may not be *the* Doctor, Dr. Lewis clearly has a deep understanding and appreciation of philosophy, and he certainly knows the Doctor! Fans of *Doctor Who*, past, present and future, will not want to miss this excellent little book. Don't let its length fool you; it's bigger on the inside!

Kevin McCain, Assistant Professor of Philosophy at the University of Alabama at Birmingham, co-editor Red Rising and Philosophy, and Author of *Evidentialism and Epistemic Justification* and *The Nature of Scientific Knowledge*.

Way of the Doctor is a must read for *Doctor Who* fans with an interest in philosophy. Professor Lewis uses his intimate knowledge of *Doctor Who* to address the thorniest of philosophical questions: how should we live? Using accessible language without dumbing down the issues, he considers the roles of wisdom, justice, openness to experience, and other factors in a life lived well. Along the way, he examines the nature of evil and the correct response to evil, the extent of human knowledge, and whether *Doctor Who* qualifies as a religion. Far from being a dry read, *Way of the Doctor* is an entertaining examination of the human condition and the light that can be thrown on it by the adventures of everyone's favorite Time Lord.

Gregory Littmann, Associate Professor of Philosophy at Southern Illinois University, Edwardsville. Contributed to several examinations of popular culture, including *Doctor Who*, Neil Gaiman, Roald Dahl, and *The Walking Dead*.

Doctor Who, and its related characters, images and themes, are the copyright © of the BBC and other related creative parties. No infringement of this copyright is either implied or intended. The views and opinions expressed in this book are those solely of the author. This book has not been prepared, authorized, or endorsed by the creators of *Doctor Who* and do not reflect the views and opinions held by the BBC or related parties.

In accordance with U.S. copyright law, title 17, Section 107, the following, which contains the reproduction of portions of particular works for criticism, comment, news reporting, teaching, scholarship, and research, is protected under the doctrine of "fair use."

Way of the Doctor:
Doctor Who's Pocketbook Guide to the Good Life

Courtland Lewis

Copyright © 2017 PhilDocBooks
All rights reserved.

ISBN: 1-544-29-8056
ISBN-13: 978-1-544-29-8054

DEDICATION

Sincerest thanks to:

Jenny, you're the best! On a personal and practical level, thank you to Kevin McCain and Paula Smithka for providing valuable feedback, R. Alan Siler and Shaun Lyon for providing a place to present and discuss my ideas, and again, Paula Smithka for being a friend, mentor, and co-editing our two volumes of *Doctor Who and Philosophy*. More abstractly, thanks to the entire creative team of *Doctor Who*, past, present, and future—Great job. A special thanks to the actors who played the Doctor—You're all my favorite! Finally, a very special thanks to my "First Doctor," John DuGard... Thanks for all of the lessons!

CONTENTS

PREFACE

INTRODUCTION 1

1 DOCTOR WHO AND THE LOVE OF WISDOM: 7

2 THE DOCTOR'S ETHICS 17

3 GETTING LOST PROPERLY: THE DOCTOR AS FLÂNEUR 36

4 AVOIDING MONSTERS: STUDIES IN EVIL 47

5 THE WRATH OF THE DOCTOR 62

6 KNOW THY DOCTOR 78

7 ON ENDINGS, AND OTHER DEPRESSING THINGS 94

8 *DOCTOR WHO* AS RELIGION 107

EPILOGUE 120

INDEX 123

PREFACE

My love of *Doctor Who* began in September of 1983, with the local broadcast of "The Sontaran Experiment" on PBS. Little did I know, but that night I would be whisked away on a journey that continues to be enthralling after thirty years. Week after week I would sit on the floor and watch. Of course, after a few years, *Doctor Who* ceased being shown on my local station, but it never completely disappeared. It was an interesting quirk of television. I felt like the only person in my town who had seen it. I would ask people from time to time, "Do you remember that show with the great theme song, long scarf, 'phone box', and tin dog?" I remember only one person responding with a "yes," and that was ten years later and the person had grown up in England.

The second major encounter with the Doctor happened in the late 80's, when the local mall's video store began selling *Doctor Who*. No longer was *Doctor Who* just some mysterious show I saw as a child, but now it was a legitimate show with its own VHS series. I now had proof that the show existed and could share my adventures with my friends.

The third major encounter happened a few years later when the Internet showed me that *Doctor Who* was a worldwide phenomenon. I found people who were just as, if not more, enthusiastic in their love for *Doctor Who*. I found books, magazines, message boards, and conventions. And then, one day, someone sent me box of VHS tapes with every Third, Fourth, and Fifth Doctor episode (recorded from PBS), along with several specials. My viewing schedule was set for the next several years. Many nights, after spending grueling hours either working at or managing a restaurant, I would come home and watch *Doctor Who*. The theme song was a celestial mantra that allowed me to relax and become lost in different times and relative dimensions.

It was during this time that I started not only trying to collect every *Doctor Who* episode, but I also began writing down quotes from the show—these quotes provided the inspiration for including quotes at the end of *Doctor Who and Philosophy: Bigger on the Inside*. I began to realize that *Doctor Who* was doing more than simply entertaining, it was teaching.

Fast-forward another decade, and *Doctor Who* was back on television. I was working towards my doctorate in philosophy, and I was offered the opportunity to submit a proposal to Open Court's Popular Culture and Philosophy Series. I hastily submitted my proposal, so much so that I misspelled 'philosophy' in the opening title. Nevertheless, I was offered a contract, and quickly brought Paula Smithka on board, along with her super knowledge of philosophy and science, to ensure the highest quality book possible.

As the book was released, I began appearing at major *Doctor Who* conventions, such as "Gallifrey One" in Los Angeles, CA and "TimeGate" (now, "WHOlanta") in Atlanta, GA. I made several friends, talked with thousands of wonderful fans, and was lucky enough to meet, talk, and share a few laughs with all sorts of people who've worked with *Doctor Who* over the years. Throughout all of this, I continued to write and think about the lessons of *Doctor Who*, and with a lot of time and effort, I completed the book you now hold in your hand.

I've worked on this book for the past five years or so, adding, cutting, and working to create something fun and accessible, yet challenging, to all audiences. I offered the book to many publishers, but all graciously said "no." The conventional wisdom is that philosophy doesn't sell. Just as the executives who thought *Doctor Who* wouldn't sell, they're wrong. I've found that *Doctor Who* fans thirst for knowledge, wisdom, and understanding. They don't mind being challenged and working through difficult problems, and I hope they enjoy the lessons I put forward within. I'm ecstatically proud of my pocketbook guide of the Doctor's lessons on the good life, and whether I sell one copy or a million, that it's produced by a small publisher (thanks PhilDocBooks!) or later picked up by someone larger, I will humbly continue to speak and teach the wisdom of *Doctor Who*. I hope you will enjoy the book half as much as me.

INTRODUCTION

When I was very young, two events and one person determined the trajectory of my life. The first event, which is actually my very first memory, was when I drank kerosene—yes, I just said "I drank *kerosene*!" As I vividly recall, I was outside of my grandparents' home and extremely thirsty. As luck would have it, I found an old coffee can of clear liquid. I could tell it was clear because I could see my reflection in the bottom. Because water is clear, I assumed the liquid was water. I was comatose for several days, kept alive in an oxygen tent. This near-death experience was a traumatic event that made me appreciate the fragility and value of life. It planted in me a seed that grew into a full-blown wonderment of life, enjoyment of laughing, and desire to ponder, know, and experience all that exists—no matter how scary.

Closely related to the wonder produced by drinking kerosene is the person and second event that greatly influenced my life—my grandfather and *Doctor Who*. Both comprise the memory of my childhood. Growing up, I spent a lot of time with my grandfather. He drove me around town visiting different hardware stores, took me on jobs (like preaching, plumbing, farming, pest control, electrical work, and locksmithing), we experimented on food, which usually involved adding different liquids to ice cream or putting Miracle Whip® on something, played an assortment of word games, he told lots of jokes, often from *Reader's Digest*®, and of course, we watched TV. It was he who introduced me to *Doctor Who*, and it was typically at his house that I watched each Saturday night on our local PBS station.

Kerosene spurred an appreciation and enjoyment of life, *Doctor Who* structured and focused the resulting passion, and my grandfather gave me a real-life example of how one should live. Watching *Doctor Who*, while lying on the floor of my grandparents' house, was like going to church—except much more interesting! Each week I found myself immersed and mystified by the strange new realities of *Doctor Who*. The episodes I remember are sacred relics of my childhood. They taught me that existence is as infinite as I want it to be, both in terms of the external world but also in terms of my internal imagination and life's potential. It challenged my understanding of right and wrong, it changed the way I understood the nature of the universe, and it gave me hope in a future where I (and everyone else) might flourish.

Living the Good Life

The purpose of this book is to show that *Doctor Who* teaches viewers a way of life, what ethicists call the *good life*. This way of life is not just some random way of living that makes you feel good. Rather, it's a prescription for how to live the best possible life, one of happiness and flourishing. Flourishing has nothing to do with pleasure or money. Instead, flourishing describes a life that has gone well, one of joy and contentment, which if you're lucky includes pleasure, but can just as easily include pain and suffering. Just as a dietician tells you how to eat properly in order to have a healthy body, ethicists attempt to describe how to live properly in order to be a healthy moral being. Achieving a healthy moral life of flourishing is the good life.

The good life in no way guarantees pleasure and ease, but it gives you a framework for how to approach a variety of situations that might arise in your life. It helps you cultivate certain tendencies that make you and everyone around you better off. As I've argued in several books and at multiple conventions, if we pay close enough attention to *Doctor Who*, we'll see it too gives us an ethic, a prescription for how to live to achieve the good life. All we need do is reflect upon and consistently describe this ethic to know how we too can flourish. My purpose is to help us along on this journey.

Ethics can be described in any number of ways, but its main purpose is to provide a coherently justified explanation for how one should live. In other words, it provides a framework for how to achieve the good life. Nevertheless, many people's first response to ethics is a negative one. They perceive it as a "parent" giving orders, and their response is, "You can't tell me what to do!" This reaction, however, is the result of a basic confusion about ethics. It's true that throughout a person's life, he or she will constantly be told what to do: parents want their kids to make good grades, politicians want you to vote for them, and culture crusaders want you to find a certain song, act, or dance disgusting. Behind most of these commands lie personal motives, subjective understandings of what is right, and sometimes simple deception. In other words, someone doesn't like something and they want you to agree with them. This is *not* ethics!

Ethics is the attempt to clearly and consistently justify moral positions, and the hallmark of ethics is the ability to provide well-thought-out reasons for why persons should act in certain ways. Ethics is more like math than art. With art, we can have wide disagreement over what is good and bad. In fact, the most disgusting artistic display imaginable (I'll let you do the imagining) might be considered "good" by others. Math, on the other hand, is the hallmark of objective reasoning, which means all rational persons will agree on the correctness of a math proof. For instance, if a rational person is given the equation "$2 + \_ = 4$," she ought to fill the blank with the number 2.

Even though there's wide disagreement in some cases, ethics provides a rational basis for making good, objectively true moral decisions. Ethics simply deals with a different set of equations. For instance, Cybermen need humans in order to increase the size of their armies, but humans are persons who have the right to be free from forced conversion into Cybermen. The equation looks something like: Cybermen's need + Human rights = $\_$. The difference between math and ethics is that there are multiple ways to fill in the blank, depending on what is considered valuable. For instance, is it pleasure, human worth and dignity, some sort of natural law, or something completely different that is valuable? Based on what's considered valuable, ethics provides a framework for how to consistently answer questions about who we should be and how we should act. Regardless of what we determine to be valuable, ethical frameworks are more akin to a mathematical system that provides a consistent set of rules, justified by reason and critical thinking, not simply opinion and desire.

So, when parents, politicians, and culture crusaders tell you to do something, they should be able to provide a set of reasons to which an intelligent and rational, yet skeptical, person might agree. If they can't, then they are *not* doing ethics. They simply want you to agree with them, and you're justified in your hesitancy to follow their orders. Of course, from time to time they might be right, and you might simply have to trust them. As Amy Pond learns during her tenure with the Doctor, he doesn't always give her good reasons for doing certain things. Instead, she must trust that what he tells her is correct. This particular problem will be discussed in Chapter 1, where I show that the Doctor is trying to teach Amy a lesson, not merely to have her follow orders. Nevertheless, as a general rule, it's better to do something based on sound reasoning, not simply because someone tells you to do it.

Asking the Right Question

Even though the Doctor doesn't always give his companions good reasons for acting during each episode, over the past fifty years, the Doctor has given viewers an ethical framework for how to live our lives. Each chapter of this book will engage in explaining what these lessons are, and each one will provide a series of reasons for why an intelligent and rational, yet skeptical, person should act a certain way. To fully understand the Doctor's lessons the reader must understand what sort of ethical question the Doctor is asking.

There are two basic questions ethics might try to answer: 1) What should I do? 2) Who should I be? The first question focuses on actions, and tries to tell you what to do within a limited set of circumstances. For instance, if you are tasked with going back in time and destroying the Daleks while they're in their infancy, should you do it? The Fourth Doctor faces this dilemma in the 1975 serial "Genesis of the Daleks." The Doctor accepts the assignment, but when the time comes to destroy them, he asks, "Do I have the right?" In other words, he's asking "what should I do?" Sarah Jane Smith refers to the evil nature of the Daleks to justify killing them, but the Doctor points to positive consequences that seem to justify their existence. What's nice about this interaction, which will be discussed in detail in Chapter 2, is that it captures two competing ethical justifications: one based on consequences, the other based on inherent value, which see consequences as irrelevant.

Answering the question of "what should I do" is a common approach to ethics, but it's not the approach typically taken by the Doctor. Instead, the Doctor answers the question: "who should I be." Though it shares similarities with the first question, the question of "who should I be" is a much broader question that deals with the entirety of a person's life. It's a question that is concerned with the character of who one is and whether or not he or she lives a life that is worth living. The question suggests that following a set of rules that tells you to perform a certain action in a particular situation isn't good enough. Instead, you should focus on bettering yourself, on making sure you're developing your character, on ensuring that you contribute to the good, and on working so that other people get what they deserve. Only then will *you*, as a moral being, flourish. When you flourish you live the *good life*. You're guided not by a set of rules, but by the type of character you want to exhibit. In other words, you don't risk your life and save the universe because an abstract rule says you should. You save the universe because you have the power to do so, and you're the kind of person who would risk her or his life for the good of yourself and others. That is "the way of the Doctor."

The Way of the Doctor

To reiterate, *Doctor Who* doesn't present a clear-cut set of rules of how to act in every situation, but it does present a coherent example of "who one should be." Over the past fifty years the Doctor has exhibited certain character traits that have taught us how we should live our lives. Chapter 1 explains how the Doctor promotes being clever and using critical thinking skills, in order to help us grow and become wiser individuals who are more aware of and engaged with our surroundings. Chapter 2 deals with the lesson he teaches us about what is right, what is just, and how to live a life that strives to ensure all creatures great and small can flourish, free from oppression and threats of extermination. Chapter 3 shows how he inspires us to step out of our comfort zone, get lost, and enjoy the wild and wonderful universe in which we find ourselves. Chapter 4 examines human desires and the nature of evil, teaching how to avoid some common ethical mistakes that might cause us to become monsters ourselves.

Since the Doctor constantly fights evil, Chapter 5 examines the Doctor's approach to punishment, vengeance, and forgiveness.

Not only does the Doctor give us examples of how to deal with the practical ethical issues covered in Chapters 1 through 5, he also engages deeper questions of human existence. More specifically, the Doctor provides insights into human knowledge, which will be discussed in Chapter 6. He also examines the meaning of human nature, death, pain, and existence, and even though these questions can create a certain amount of angst, the Doctor's adventures give us hope that we'll survive and grow stronger from our experiences. An examination of these existential vulnerabilities, framed in terms of the Doctor's supposed hatred of endings, will be discussed in Chapter 7. As a result of the Doctor's engagement with human nature and existence, *Doctor Who* has recently been granted the status of "religion" by some. If religion is understood as a set of ritualistic human practices that promote a specific set of beliefs and behaviors, then *Doctor Who* might just deserve such a status. This book argues that the Doctor presents us with a way of living the good life. So, is granting *Doctor Who* the status of "religion" justified? Chapter 8 will attempt to answer this question.

My hope is that each chapter will engage readers young and old, whether you're on your first body or your 12th regeneration. No previous knowledge of ethics or *Doctor Who* is necessary; though having some knowledge of both will enhance your journey. The lessons of *Doctor Who* are accessible to everyone, and so I will present them in a way that all readers can understand. For me, *Doctor Who* does more than just entertain. It enlightens and motivates, and I hope that this book will do the same. I'm ready to get started. I hope you are too. So, let the journey begin—Allons-y!

References:
Episodes:
Doctor Who
    "Genesis of the Daleks" (1975)

1

DOCTOR WHO and **THE LOVE OF WISDOM**

> …It was a better life. I don't mean all the travelling and seeing aliens and spaceships and things. That don't matter. The Doctor showed me a better way of living your life…You don't just give up. You don't just let things happen. You make a stand. You say "no." You have the guts to do what's right when everyone else just runs away…
>
> —Rose ("The Parting of the Ways," 2005)
>
> When you're a kid they tell you it's all…grow up, get a job, get a house, have a kid, and that's it. But the truth is: the world is so much stranger than that. It's so much darker…and so much madder…and so much *better*.
>
> —Elton Pope ("Love & Monsters," 2006)

To some, the Doctor is simply a wandering vagabond with a group of companions, stumbling around the galaxy and having adventures that usually involve saving a species, a planet, and occasionally, the entire Universe. I held a similar view when I began watching *Doctor Who* in the early 80's, and must admit it remains a driving force behind what keeps me coming back for more. The adventures, the unknown, and the spectacle are all important parts of *Doctor Who*, but as Rose and Elton suggest in the passages quoted above, *Doctor Who* is about so much more. The Doctor teaches a way of life. In everything he does, the Doctor engages the deep recesses of what it means to be human, and he exemplifies a way of life that is worthy of living. The Doctor is by no means perfect, but as each chapter of this book suggests, he presents a way of living that is worthy of emulation.

The first step towards living a good life is to learn the skill of critical thinking. Luckily, it's one of the main lessons of *Doctor Who*. Of course, critical thinking can be approached in a number of ways. First, it can be viewed as a technique to be employed when performing a certain task. For instance, imagine you're in the episode "Blink" (2007), and a weeping angel has transported you to the past *with* the TARDIS. But without the Doctor's knowledge of "Timey Wimey, Wibbly Wobbly...stuff," it's up to you to figure out how to fly the TARDIS back to the Doctor. After your initial shock, you would need to use your critical thinking skills to solve the problem—good luck!

Thankfully, most of us won't be asked to solve such a difficult problem, but it still illustrates how critical thinking skills are used on an occasional basis to solve particular problems. For good or ill, the fact is, people rarely go around in a constant state of analyzing their surroundings. Instead, we often have our "auto-pilot" engaged, until we need to employ careful and explicit critical thinking to solve a problem, from working the daily Jumble® to figuring out how to pay the bills at the end of the month.

Some people do, however, make a habit of analyzing themselves and their surroundings. They do it so much that critical thinking simply becomes a way of life. Philosophers are notorious for not "switching it off," which is why people don't often equate 'party animal' with 'philosopher'. In fact, there's a tendency for some people to become nervous when around philosophers, like we're Cybermen just waiting for our chance to upgrade them! For the most part philosophers are harmless, but their love of wisdom can prevent them from simply going with the flow of things, without thoroughly analyzing what's being said or what's occurring in their surroundings. Of course, this should remind you of someone else—the Doctor, for the Doctor's approach to life is based on constant, never-ceasing critical thinking.

Living with the Doctor

Philosophy comes from the Greek *philo* (love) and *sophia* (wisdom). So, philosophy is fundamentally the "love of wisdom," and it's this love of wisdom that grounds critical thinking as a way of life. To see why this sort of life is desirable, let's look at how it occurs in everyday life.

My wife is constantly asked, "What is it like to be married to a philosopher?" I like to say, "It's like living with the Doctor, minus the time travel and regenerations." Of course, a more accurate answer, and the one my wife gives, is that philosophers have a desire to understand everything, so they ask lots of questions and want really clear and precise answers. And when I say, "everything," I mean *everything*: God, human nature, beauty, right and wrong, the inner-workings of science, logic, mathematics, the nature of reality beyond human experience, personal identity, and among many other things, how humans can have knowledge of any of these things. To gain an understanding of such things, philosophers use critical thinking skills like logic, conceptual analysis, and abstract reasoning. They are much like a scientist looking for the best possible explanations based on what we can know. In fact, until the 19th century "scientists" were called "natural philosophers," because they were philosophers engaged in explaining nature (i.e. the natural world). Anyone who has taken a course on theoretical physics knows that it's more akin to philosophy than what many would call traditional empirical science. Regardless of the name we give different fields of study, the ground on which these fields of study are based is critical thinking.

The critical thinking that is the hallmark of philosophy requires that people continually reflect on their beliefs and actions and become aware of the ways in which both affect others. It also requires them to be willing to buck outdated traditions when counterevidence shows those traditions to be wrong. As Thomas Kuhn's book *The Structures of Scientific Revolutions* illustrates nicely, the nature of critical thinking requires that we reject beliefs when counterevidence makes accepting such beliefs a matter of holding on to a convoluted, inconsistent, and overly complex worldview. It's this very feature of critical thinking that makes being a critical thinker difficult and, for some, extremely scary. Nevertheless, it's what a true lover of wisdom strives to do.

Philosophy, *fantastic*

Like philosophy, *Doctor Who* challenges people to reflect on the nature of existence, though it does it in a slightly more exciting way than *most* college philosophy courses. Regardless of people's memory of their college philosophy class, philosophy is a fascinating, exciting, and sometimes spiritual enterprise. It can change the course of your life and make you see the world and yourself in ways you never imagined. To see this, let's take a closer look.

So far, philosophy has been defined as the love of wisdom, but if you ask a philosopher, "what's 'philosophy'?", you're bound to receive as many different answers as you would if you asked a *Doctor Who* fan, "who's your favorite Doctor?" or "what's your favorite episode?" There's simply no easy, straightforward answer to give that's universally satisfactory. 'Philosophy' is the love of wisdom, but really, it's so much more. Socrates (c. 469 BCE-399 BCE), through the dialogues of Plato (428/7 BCE-348/7 BCE), said that philosophy is that which aids one's choosing of the good life (*Republic*), the greatest of arts (*Phaedo*), a sense of wonder (*Theaetetus*), the most important way to prepare for death (*Crito*), and the love of real knowledge (*Republic*). Of course, none of these descriptions completely describes philosophy. What's needed is to take these descriptions of philosophy and combine them with a discussion of what philosophy is *not*.

Opposed to philosophy is sophistry, which is the practice of rhetoric performed by the "sophists" in Socrates's time. Besides charging for their services, sophists were not concerned with truth. They only cared about making their patrons "happy" by helping them win arguments. To win arguments, sophists engaged in rhetoric, which Plato's *Gorgias* defines as the art of persuasive speaking. Without going into the finer details of the dialogue, Socrates engages in a discussion with Gorgias, a great rhetorical orator, about the nature of Gorgias's profession as a sophist. Based on Gorgias's answers, Socrates makes an important distinction between what we would call *teaching* vs. *persuasion*.

Persuasion is presented as a power that orators have over

others—to make individuals and groups succumb to the orator's will. As Aristotle examines in detail in *On Rhetoric*, a rhetorician uses a variety of tools and techniques (words, historical examples, emotions, pauses, etc.) to rouse an audience's emotions and convince them of what's wrong and right. The goal of such orators is to win an argument at any cost, whether by lying, deceiving, or obfuscation. Furthermore, it fails to produce any sort of reliable knowledge. The only "knowledge" you gain is the propaganda that the orator wants you to believe. For a good example, think of your favorite sleazy politician, or better yet, the Master.

Imagine if the Master needed your help to carry out one of his evil plans to destroy the Earth. He must somehow convince you that it's in your best interest to help him destroy the Earth (if he doesn't just hypnotize you first), and the most effective way for him to do this is to play off of your fears and emotions. By using your fears and emotions he keeps you from using your critical thinking skills. As a result, you can't think clearly about what's the best course of action. This is the nature of rhetoric. Just like a cook who takes a rotten piece of meat and seasons it in such a way that makes it taste delicious, rhetoric has the ability to take a falsehood, or a half-truth, and presents it in such a way that you believe it's true.

Such beliefs have no justification or grounding. For instance, the *belief* that you must help the Master is only grounded on the fact that the Master told you so, and as we all know, you can't trust the Master. Your trust in the Master is unreliable because the Master is unreliable, and if you applied any real critical thinking to the issue, you should see that your trust in the Master and resulting belief won't hold up to scrutiny.

Instead of your belief grounded on something more certain, like a critically thought-out plan on how to save the Earth, your belief is based on the Master's persuasive abilities. The result of his unreliability is that your belief is unreliable too. Still, the Master is effective because he knows how to manipulate people. He knows your interests and concerns, and he uses them to persuade you to help further his goals. It's this knack of persuasion, by creating false beliefs in individuals, which allows him to gain control over so many subjects. Even his use of hypnosis, which was prominent in the Classic Series, is merely a form of subliminal persuasion.

You shouldn't trust anyone who's only concerned with

persuasion. They don't care about you or the truth. They only care about winning, being "right," and having you agree with them. So, whether it's politics, religion, or world domination, critical thinking tells you to look for and trust persons who are concerned with truth, especially if they have a successful methodology—like, logic—for discovering the truth.

The Right Path

What Socrates refers to as teaching, on the other hand, has a very different goal than that of rhetoric. Teaching is the attempt to pass knowledge from one individual to another, or to help individuals reach some understanding about truth, usually via the method of critical thinking. It's not concerned with "winning" an argument, nor is it concerned with causing interlocutors to conform to the will of the teacher. Teaching is about engaging others in a dialogue, whether verbal or through actions. This engagement helps "students" arrive at justified *true* beliefs about a particular idea or subject matter.

Opposed to the Master's use of rhetoric, the Doctor is a teacher. He's a teacher because he's dedicated to truth. Even though he occasionally deceives, which he admits to, he does so to teach important lessons: as he says to Amy Pond in the 2010 episode "Flesh and Stone," "If I always told you the truth, I wouldn't need you to trust me." Of course, a skeptical reader might complain that such an explanation just shows that the Doctor is at best parentalistic, and at worst, no better than the Master. Such a complaint would be too hasty, for the Doctor isn't merely a parent who knows best, nor is he just interested in getting his own way. If we examine the Doctor's actions over the entire series we see that he's doing more than saying, "Trust me, because I know best." Instead, he's doing something much deeper—he's helping his companions (and viewers) grow and learn from their adventures.

The type of truth that the Doctor is interested in involves helping people be autonomous (i.e. self-governing). The Doctor isn't interested in simply telling us how to live. Instead, he wants us to engage in living, and from this, arrive at a set of principles for how to properly order our life. In other words, he isn't preaching to us about how to live a certain way, he's trying to teach us a better way to live, by having us engage in actually *living*. To accomplish his task, the

Doctor must sometimes withhold certain details in order to allow us to work through the problem. Just like a teacher who gives you a test, asks you a series of questions, and/or presents you with a difficult thought experiment, the Doctor is trying to test your mastery and understanding of a certain set of material. He's not doing it for selfish reasons. Instead, he wants you to learn and grow, to take the things you've learned and to use them to more properly govern yourself. The task of the Doctor is much different than the Master. Not only does it require much more work, and a larger amount of patience, it requires a dedication to something more substantial than being right. It requires a dedication to truth and seeing others grow through the process of coming to understand what such truth implies for one's life.

From the above discussion, we can conclude that it's not persuasion in itself that is bad, but it's the intention of the persuader that matters. Teachers, like the Doctor, often persuade, but their type of persuasion is based on the intention of helping you become a better, more autonomous person who lives a life of truth, consistency, and integrity. Whereas, people like the Master, who uses persuasion to flatter, gain power, and for other selfish reasons don't care about you, truth, or anyone besides themselves and their own self-gain.

According to Socrates, true philosophers are teachers, and if we combine the characteristics of teachers with the characteristics of philosophy mentioned above, then we will have a much clearer understanding of philosophy. Philosophy is a dedication to self-reflection, truth, and consistency, which as Socrates suggests, is necessary for living the good life and having knowledge.

As a result, philosophy is many things to many people: it's a way of life, a tool to achieve consistency and order in one's life, the search for knowledge and wisdom, and a spiritual quest. Philosophy defies easy characterization because it's concerned with wisdom and understanding, and these pursuits require that it be partially engaged with every field of study and every aspect of existence. As a result, philosophy is a little bit of everything to everyone, and that's good.

Doctor Who as Philosophy

As seen above, philosophy is a way of life that promotes the thoughtful engagement of the world. I have suggested that *Doctor Who* promotes a similar lifestyle. Let us look at a few examples that support this suggestion.

Most viewers know that *Doctor Who* began as an educational show. On a much deeper level it provides us with an example of someone who is dedicated to discovering truth, promoting consistency, and fostering integrity, all of which are components of the philosophical act of *teaching*. *Doctor Who* challenges people in three particular ways: 1) to be reflective about one's own life and the ways in which one reasons; 2) to be reflective about how one treats others; and 3) always be willing change one's views in light of new evidence. From the very beginning, the Doctor took viewers on adventures to historical places like Rome ("The Romans," 1965), the Aztec Empire ("The Aztecs," 1964), and on a journey with Marco Polo ("Marco Polo," 1964). The show wasn't merely concerned with winning over audiences with exciting stories about time travel, which it did, but it was concerned with teaching the audience about strange new places and aliens, and that we should respect their differences and appropriately adjust how we act around them.

As illustrated in Brian Robb's insightful book *Timeless Adventures: How Doctor Who Conquered TV*, the attempt to teach the audience can be seen throughout the series, and most of the lessons are not historical, they're ethical, moral, and sometimes spiritual. It presents viewers with ways of understanding complex issues, and gives them the tools to reflect upon and arrive at consistent philosophical conclusions. For example, "The Green Death" (1973) teaches viewers about the importance of environmental stewardship, but it never lays down dictates for exactly how one should treat the environment. Episodes like "The Silurians" (1970) teach viewers about coexisting with other species. "The End of the World" (2005) raises questions about justice, death, and self-importance. And throughout every episode, viewers are challenged to respect life in whatever form, do what is right, and to live life to its fullest. The 2011 two-story arc "The Almost People" and "The Rebel Flesh" challenges viewers to consider what it means to be part of the social and moral community of equals. The continuing story arc involving the Time War, seen throughout the New Series, directly engages the themes of war, violence, nonviolence, and genocide. From these and countless other examples that could be provided, *Doctor Who* is so much more than a mere science fiction show. It's a teaching tool that's actively engaged in challenging viewers to think, consider how they would act in certain situations, and what proper course of action is best for everyone.

Doctor Who presents deep philosophical investigations that are designed to teach and challenge viewers to arrive at their own truthful and consistent conclusions. *Doctor Who* challenges us all to consider how we view our own lives, how we treat others, and how we understand what counts as truth by presenting us with philosophical case studies in the form of episodic television. It's a never-ending process. As we watch from season to season we test the Doctor's consistency. Can he remain consistent while being forced to deal with Cybermen, Daleks, Sontarans, Ice Warriors, the Master, Zygons, Jagrafess, the surviving brain of the villainous Time Lord Morbius, Abzorbaloffs, Sea Devils, Slitheen, Vashta Nerada, the Silence and the Weeping Angels? From watching and critically engaging the Doctor's way of life, we then engage and learn whether or not our own moral beliefs are consistent. We learn and grow from this engagement, so when we're forced to deal with other people, strangers, and enemies that actually exist here on Earth, we'll know how best to act.

"Ah, Doctor. We Know You by Reputation"

The Doctor has a reputation because of his non-stop critical thinking and the excitement that comes from living. It's easy to get caught up in one's own way of seeing things, and to try and force others to see the world exactly the same way. *Doctor Who* tries to get us to live life differently. It calls us to engage ourselves and the world around us, to change the way we see the world and the way we treat others. It makes us consider the possibility that we might achieve "the impossible." *Doctor Who* shows us that we, and the world in which we live, is larger on the inside than on the outside, and that it's this Time And Relative Dimension in *all Spaces* that makes the world so much stranger, so much darker, so much madder, and so much *better*! It's from all of this that it teaches us to strive for something greater: a life of critical thinking lived according to the good.

Notes:
This chapter was inspired and influenced by a similar chapter, which originally appeared as "Philosophy, *Fantastic!*" *Doctor Who and Philosophy: Bigger on the Inside*, edited by Courtland Lewis and Paula Smithka. Chicago: Open Court, 2010.

References:
Episodes:
Doctor Who
       "Marco Polo" (1964)
       "The Aztecs" (1964)
       "The Romans" (1965)
       "The Silurians" (1970)
       "The Green Death" (1973)
       "The End of the World" (2005)
       "The Parting of the Ways" (2005)
       "Love and Monsters" (2006)
       "Blink" (2007)
       "Flesh and Stone" (2010)
       "The Almost People" (2011)
       "The Rebel Flesh" (2011)

Authors:

Aristotle. (2001). *The Basic Works of Aristotle*. Edited by Richard McKeon. Introduction by C.D.C Reeve. New York: The Modern Library; first published by Random House, 1941.

Kuhn, Thomas S. (1996). *The Structure of Scientific Knowledge*, 3rd edition. Chicago and London: University of Chicago Press; first published, 1962.

Plato. (1999). *The Collected Dialogues of Plato, Including the Letters*, 17th edition. Edited by Edith Hamilton and Huntington Cairns. New Jersey: Princeton University Press; first published, 1961.

Robb, Brian. (2009). *Timeless Adventures: How Doctor Who Conquered TV*. London: Kamera Books.

2

THE DOCTOR'S ETHICS

As we learn about each other, so we learn about ourselves.

—First Doctor ("The Edge of Destruction," 1963)

As briefly discussed in the Introduction, morals are those feelings, beliefs, and intuitions of right and wrong you have in your gut, and ethics is the systematic attempt to prove whether or not you're justified in holding those moral beliefs. We all have beliefs about what's wrong and right, and in fact, it's quite common to hear someone say something like, "There's no wrong or right, because we all have different opinions." For ethicists, this statement is simply false, for the straightforward reason that just because we disagree, it doesn't mean that there is no truth. Even ethicists who claim there are no moral truths beyond cultural conventions and personal subjective feelings, will often use language and cultural conventions to ground some sort of contextual moral truth. Books have been written on the subject of moral truth, but let me stop us here, since this isn't a chapter about the nature of language and the basis of morality. This, however, is a chapter about the Doctor's ethics, and if you've watched much *Doctor Who*, you know that the Doctor believes there's a wrong and a right that applies to every being in the universe. So, for the Doctor there is moral truth. What is more, since the Doctor continually holds other beings to a moral standard, it's safe to assume that he believes there's some sort of ethical system that ties all of our moral beliefs together. That's what we want to find and examine.

Before starting, and to help clear up any confusion, let me make some clarifying statements. First, the term 'theory' in 'ethical theory' is used in a technical sense, not in the "loosey goosey" sense used by some to mean "what I think" or "my gut feeling." For instance, I might claim to have a "theory" about who will be the next Doctor. I might even come up with some fancy explanation for how I arrived at my "theory." No matter how knowledgeable I am of *Doctor Who*, such a claim is just mere conjecture, and isn't the way ethicists (or scientists) use the term 'theory'. Compare my claim about the next Doctor to the "theory of gravity." Even though there's a lot we don't know about gravity, our theory is pretty darn consistent. If you drop an object, no matter its weight, it'll drop at a crisp 9.8 m/s^2—unless acted on by an outside force, of course. Ethical *theories* attempt to provide the same sort of consistent justification as scientific *theories*. They might not be perfect, and there's still work to be done, but contrary to popular opinion, most ethical theories do a nice job of consistently explaining many of our moral intuitions.

Unlike scientific theories that rely on observable data, ethical theories typically deal with the unobservable. For instance, when you see someone stabbed, the observable data is that they were stabbed. Ethicists, on the other hand, aren't interested in the fact a person was stabbed. They're interested in what *should* have happened. For example, a typical ethicist would say "he should not have been stabbed," but to say such a thing is to say, "What occurred in the world *should* not have occurred; the world *should* be different." This is what ethicists call a "normative" claim, which is easy to spot due to the use of the word 'should', and sometimes 'ought'. Normative words like 'should' and 'ought' recognize the world is one way, but suggest it should be different. Ethical theories combine normative claims to create a consistent explanation of how the world should be. The more complete and consistent the explanation, the stronger the ethical theory.

The second feature of ethics readers should understand is that disagreements between competing ethical theories is usually the result of what each theory values. All ethical theories use some account of *value* to distinguish what is good and right, from what is bad and wrong. We'll look at several below, one that values pleasure, one that values rationality and duties, one that values virtuous character, one that values caring relationships, and one that values needs. Once an ethicist determines what is morally valuable, they then construct a consistent set of moral guidelines based on language, thought experiments, and the conceptual analysis of moral issues to arrive at a justified ethical theory. Based on this sort of analytical process, ethicists work to determine what is 'good' and what is 'bad'.

Like 'love', however, 'good' is one of those words used so often we seldom take time to think about what it means. There's a *good* reason for this: 'Good' is a complex word. There are good friends, good pizzas, and good *Doctor Who* episodes. Yet, the 'good' in each of these instances refers to something completely different. The qualities that make a "good" pizza are much different than what makes a "good" friend or "good" *Doctor Who* episode. So, how do we arrive at an understanding of 'good' that captures its varied uses?

In the face of such a task, some people will simply claim that 'good' is a matter of subjective opinion: I think it's good, so it's good. To a certain extent such an explanation is correct. For instance, most fans agree that Neil Gaiman's 2011 episode "The Doctor's Wife" is a good episode, but disagree over the merits of his 2013 episode "Nightmare in Silver." These sorts of disagreements appear to be based merely on personal preference. Of course, fans will point to all sorts of "evidence" to support their position as an objective truth, but ultimately the "goodness" of both episodes is not only subjective, but the use of 'good' in these sorts of statements relates to the concept of beauty, *not* morality. For the majority of people, and in most situations, 'good' is used merely as an expression of personal tastes, like favorite color, favorite Doctor, favorite pizza toppings, and so on. None of these uses obviously involve a moral issue, so it's okay to say there's no right answer to the question of which pizzas and episodes are good and which are bad; or you could say that all such answers are right. Your love of fish fingers and custard on your pizza is based on your subjective tastes, and unless you physically force or coerce your friends into eating your concoction, it's not a moral issue. However, once you bring the harm and welfare of others into the scenario, it now becomes a moral discussion. It's moved from your own tastes, to the harm of others.

Morality's use of 'good'—and in this instance, we can use 'ethics' and 'morality' interchangeably—says something about how a moral agent treats, or fails to treat, themselves and other moral agent. See how I used 'moral agent' instead of the more common 'person'. Even the word 'person' has the moral implication of valuing rationality over something like the ability to feel pleasure and pain. I told you ethics is tricky. Back to my original point, morality describes a relationship between moral agents. It discusses how we should or should not act throughout our lives—hence, the term 'the good life'. As we move forward in this chapter, you'll see there are a variety of different explanations about what is valuable and what is good. However, just because there's disagreement over which account is correct, it doesn't follow that there's no correct account. We might disagree over the appearance of John Cleese in "City of Death" (1979), but that doesn't mean one of us isn't right. We just have to watch the episode, or at least that's the most fun way to settle the disagreement. As previously mentioned, due to the Doctor's actions, thoughts, and words, we're assuming there is a correct account of morality, even if we're unable to completely understand and describe such an ethic. So, to determine his ethic, we have the fun task of watching *Doctor Who*.

As you can tell just from this opening section, ethics is complex and difficult—just like the Doctor. To help make sense of the Doctor's ethic, and to ensure the topic is properly covered, two chapters will be dedicated to examining the Doctor's ethic. This chapter will provide a theoretical explanation of how the Doctor understands the moral universe, and Chapter 3 will discuss the more practical application of his ethic. So, with the above in mind, let's explore some prominent moral theories and see which ones are incapable of serving as the Doctor's ethic and which ones are dynamic enough to ground it.

Getting In The Thick Of Things

If the theoretical grounding for the Doctor's ethic of the good life can be summed up in a brief statement, then a motto from existentialist, environmentalist, and outdoorsman Forrest Wood, Jr.

sums it up nicely, saying, "I believe in 'getting in the thick of things'." For Wood, "getting in the thick of things" challenges us to act, make decisions, change the world around us, change ourselves, and learn first-hand how to answer life's most perplexing questions. For the Doctor, "getting in the thick of things" means that he interferes with every person, society, species, and world, past, present, and future. Nothing in the entire space-time continuum is safe from the Doctor's interference. So, what sort of ethical theory grounds this life? To help in this enormous task, I'll limit our discussion to the "life of pleasure," "life of duty," "life of virtue," "life of care," and "life of needs." Also, since many of these theories have long and complex pedigrees, I'll only be able to provide a survey of their most relevant features. For a more in-depth discussion of these theories, read the authors cited below or see my article "Understanding Peace Within Contemporary Moral Theory," featured in *Philosophia*. With that said, let's begin with the life of pleasure.

A Life Of Pleasure

The experientially satisfying life is based on consequentialist reasoning, most commonly referred to as utilitarianism. Developed by Jeremy Bentham and John Stuart Mill, and prominently supported by contemporary philosophers like Peter Singer, utilitarianism is an ends-based theory of ethics that maintains what's morally right is that which produces the most pleasure over pain, all things considered. In other words, when faced with a decision of how to act in a particular situation, a utilitarian will choose the course of action that produces the most pleasure for the most people, while at the same time minimizing the amount of pain produced, for all those affected by the act. A good example of this occurs in "Genesis of the Daleks" (1975), where Sarah Jane Smith uses consequentialist reasoning to argue that the Doctor should, in fact, eradicate the Daleks, saying: "Think of all the suffering there will be if you don't [kill the Daleks]." However, the Doctor refuses to accept such consequences as a grounds for what he should do; instead, he bases his reasons on the existence of rights, asking: "Do I have the right?"

Think about how Sarah Jane's and the Doctor's statements differ. Sarah Jane is looking at the consequences of letting the Daleks live, specifically the suffering that will occur. The Doctor, on the other hand, refers to the moral concept of a "right," which suggests the consequences don't matter. At another point in their discussion, the Doctor even considers the possible consequences, and suggests Sarah Jane's calculations might be wrong; that the Daleks might actually bring about more pleasure than pain. Regardless of the merits of each position, one of the key moral insights of the conversation is that utilitarianism is based on a conception of *instrumental worth*, where the value of individuals—in this case, Daleks—depends solely on the amount of pleasure over pain they might produce. Since the Daleks cause a lot of unnecessary pain, according to utilitarianism, they have very little (if any) moral worth.

To help illustrate, imagine the following. You're a security guard at a warehouse that just happens to be storing all of Van Gogh's original artwork. One night the Daleks attack the warehouse, setting it ablaze—"Van Gogh is an enemy of the Daleks!!!" You run to save the art, but when you get to the crate, you find a homeless person unconscious on the floor. You can only save one, so which do you save? In terms of instrumental worth, Van Gogh's artwork has more value than a homeless person. Think of the millions of people affected negatively by the loss of Van Gogh's original art, then think of how few will be affected by the loss of a single homeless person. (Nothing against homeless people. Heck, I was once homeless. If you like, imagine it's a philosophy teacher.) The point is the pain caused by losing Van Gogh's masterpieces will be much greater than the loss of one person. According to instrumental worth, the value of each thing is determined by its ability to produce pleasure over pain, and in this case, Van Gough wins—In your face, Daleks!

Utilitarianism, then, suggests a way of life in which a person's actions and decisions should bring about the most good and the least amount of bad for all individuals affected by one's decisions. As positives, utilitarianism has the advantages of being intuitively plausible and easy to apply to a wide variety of situations. As drawbacks, it's commonly misapplied by people who give their pleasure more weight than others, and it doesn't handle issues of justice very well. Justice implies a type of *inherent worth*, where a moral agent is valuable regardless of the consequences. Justice claims it's wrong to punish innocent people, yet utilitarianism can justify punishing an innocent person, if doing so increases the amount of pleasure over pain.

Even if some readers find utilitarianism attractive, the Doctor is not a utilitarian. For one, utilitarianism doesn't require any engagement with the world or other individuals. Think of the Time Lords: they spend a large majority of their time on Gallifrey, contemplating and studying the intricacies of time (at least they did before the Great Time War), and they promote and practice a policy of non-interference. In *Anarchy, State, and Utopia*, Robert Nozick provides an interesting thought experiment designed to criticize utilitarianism that is analogous to the Time Lords' policy of non-interference. Nozick asks readers to imagine an "experience machine" in which a person could live his entire life. The machine is capable of sustaining life and simulating any number of pleasures and experiences, while at the same time preventing its user from ever feeling pain. According to utilitarianism, then, we should choose to live our life in the experience machine. We could live our lives vicariously through a type of mediated experience, just like the Time Lords, never having to face the fears and difficulties of "real" life. This is exactly the sort of life the Doctor rejects, holding that engagement in the "real" world is always better than life in the "fake" world of an experience machine—no matter how awful life is sometimes.

What is more, the Doctor rejects the notion that humans (and most other entities) only have instrumental worth. He constantly stands up for the *rights* of others, making sure they get what they deserve. For such a position to make sense, he must hold an ethical position grounded on some sort of inherent worth. So, regardless of the individual merits of utilitarianism, the Doctor doesn't see it as the good life.

A Life of Duty

A life of duty is commonly referred to as duty ethics, and is most prominently associated with Immanuel Kant. As the name suggests, duty ethics is based on a notion of moral duties, grounded in the inherent worth of rational autonomous agents. Unlike utilitarianism, duty ethics doesn't care about consequences. It seeks to determine what sort of duties a rational moral agent has to other moral agents. As a result, duty ethics focuses on the rational abilities (or capacities) of individuals. If an individual is rationally autonomous, which means they're capable of rationally governing themselves (or at a minimum, have the potential of rational autonomy), then they have inherent moral worth. So, if we look at the same case discussed with utilitarianism, duty ethics says you have a duty to save the homeless person, since they're a person with inherent moral worth. Art has no moral worth, though it might have some other type, like aesthetic worth.

From the outset, duty ethics is a strong contender for the Doctor's ethic. We've already said the Doctor accepts inherent worth. As he proclaims in "A Christmas Carol" (2010), "900 years of time and space, and I've never met anyone who wasn't important." The Doctor's use of 'important' signifies his understanding of the inherent worth of all beings, even enemies. We've already mentioned his unwillingness to destroy the Daleks in "Genesis of the Daleks," but at the end of "Journey's End" (2008) he desperately tries to save his arch-enemy Davros. He also tries to save is arch-nemesis the Master in "Last of the Time Lords" (2007). This matches up with duty ethics, which would say all rational autonomous beings have moral worth, and should be saved. The big questions is: What about non-rational beings?

It's true that the Doctor typically focuses on saving rational autonomous beings, but he also sees value in the environment ("The Green Death," 1973), mindless slaves, like the Ood in "The Impossible Planet/The Satan Pit," and mechanical robots, like K-9 ("The Invisible Enemy," 1977) and D84 ("The Robots of Death," 1977). These, and other examples, illustrate how the Doctor values all life. Granted, it's later revealed that the Ood are rationally autonomous, but when we first meet them they're basically mindless automatons. What is more, some readers might want to argue that K-9 and D84 are rational beings, and they'd be correct, but they aren't rationally autonomous. If we set aside our sentimentality, they're just robots that can be turned off, replicated, and thrown away at will. The Fourth Doctor seems to have a ready supply of K-9s that he keeps in the TARDIS until he's ready to use them ("The Invasion of Time"). I don't know of any other companion that he keeps in a box in the TARDIS.

Why is this important? According to duty ethics, moral worth is grounded in some sort of rational capacity, yet the Doctor values more than a being's rational capacities. Even with robots like K-9, he genuinely loves and is excited by his friend ("School Reunion"), and though he recognizes it as a robot, he respects its decisions of whether or not to sacrifice itself for others. Duty ethics would have a difficult time morally explaining such sentimental feelings. More importantly, children aren't fully-rational autonomous beings, but the Doctor always comes when a child cries ("The Beast Below," 2010 and "Night Terrors," 2011). Duty ethics, too easily, allows for non-rational (or non-fully-rational) beings to be excluded from moral consideration. Since the Doctor sees inherent moral value in a wide range of entities, rational, semi-rational, and non-rational, a life of duty falls short of the richness illustrated in the Doctor's ethic.

A Life of Virtue

The life of virtue, sometimes called virtue or character ethics is one of our oldest moral traditions. First developed in Ancient Greece, it regained popularity over the past fifty years or so, mainly because of some of the issues noted with the two previous moral theories. The life of virtue is based on the ancient concept of *eudaimonism*. *Eudaimonism* is simply the Greek term for happiness, or well-being, and was used by Ancient Greek philosophers, like Aristotle, the Stoics, and early Christian philosophers, but also, over the past several decades, has grown in popularity amongst contemporary ethicists like Alasdair MacIntyre.

One of the most important things to keep straight is that virtue ethicists use the term 'happiness' to describe something very specific, and should not be confused with 'pleasure'. Pleasure is a state of having one's senses stimulated in a positive way. Happiness, on the other hand, is something much more complex, and requires a set of life experiences to be capable of determining whether or not an individual is happy. According to Aristotle, all humans strive towards happiness, so a rational autonomous person would naturally do what best-ensures a life of happiness. What best-ensures living such a life? For virtue ethicists, living a life of *virtue*—the active engagement of making good, moderate moral decisions—is the best way to ensure a person achieves happiness.

Stated differently, to best-ensure achieving happiness a person must consider her entire life and how her decisions affect that life. The process is similar to that of utilitarianism, but instead of looking at how to produce particular instances of pleasure or desire-satisfaction, virtue ethicists are concerned with producing an *entire life* that is well-lived and, therefore, happy. Another feature to draw special attention to is that the life of virtue is a life of *activity*. Individuals are involved in the process of becoming "happy." Happiness is not a thing, like money, that can be possessed; rather, it's a process of making good decisions. Happiness, then, is the product of living a well-lived life, or what we can call the virtuous life; and living one's life virtuously means that one carefully considers one's actions and decisions in order to produce a happy life out of the random events one is constantly confronted with.

For some, the biggest shortcoming of the life of virtue is that it focuses too much on individual character. So, when a moral agent considers what she should do, it's a consideration of what will lead to *her flourishing*. Sure, a virtue ethicist will consider others, but at its core is a self-interested consideration of personal happiness. As a result, sacrificing for others can only be explained in terms of a temporary sympathy for others, or as something heroic. Heroism is seen as performing an action that goes beyond what's morally required, but that is *necessary* in order to accomplish some goal. I'll talk more about heroism in the next section, so let's focus our attention on sympathy. To see how this plays out, imagine a different ending to "The Caves of Androzani" (1984). Peri becomes sick from spectrox toxaemia. The Doctor doesn't have a cure, and instead of making himself sick, he rushes Peri to the nearest hospital, where instead of a fairly quick death, Peri suffers over a period of several years. What should the Doctor do? Should he spend the next several years at Peri's bedside, suffering along with her, or should he grieve with her for a short period and then move on to some new adventure? What should Peri do? Should she welcome the Doctor's beside companionship, or should she tell him to go on with his life?

This is one of the toughest situations for a person who strives to live the life of virtue. To be happy, a person can't live a life of constant suffering, especially when that suffering is *unnecessary*. At some point such a life would prevent flourishing, and without flourishing, the life of virtue falls apart. So the answers to our above questions are that the Doctor should feel pity and sympathy for Peri, and maybe he should visit with her for a short period of time, but he shouldn't be her bedside partner, nor should he continually remind himself of her suffering by visiting often. He should move on with his life. Peri, too, should want the same for the Doctor. As a friend, she doesn't want him to suffer, and in order to avoid suffering, she should prompt him to continue his journeys.

The conceptual difference is that the life of virtue requires sympathy, the feeling of pain *for* someone who's suffering, not the feeling of pain *with* the suffering. It's a subtle, but important difference, for it's the difference between sympathy (feeling pain for) and compassion (feeling pain for *and* with).

The role of compassion within the life of virtue is still hotly debated among ethicists, and some forms of virtue ethicists have attempted to incorporate suffering into the life of virtue. We even see the Doctor struggle with sympathy vs. compassion, but there can be no doubt that the Doctor suffers *with* the people for whom he cares, not merely *for* them. To see the Doctor's compassion, readers need to look no further than the Eleventh Doctor's final episode "The Time of the Doctor" (2013), where he gives up traveling and adventuring in order to spend the rest of his life protecting the people of Christmas from certain death. It wasn't necessary for him to stay, nor did he have any relationship to the people of Christmas or Trenzalore. Yet, his compassion led him to suffer with the people of Christmas, and even though it cost him many years and a leg in the process, he found a way to flourish. So, if the life of virtue lacks compassion, and for good or ill I will assume it does, it's safe to conclude that the Doctor doesn't accept virtue (at least in its Classical sense) as the good life. I'll return to this discussion in a few pages.

A Life of Care

The fourth conception of the good life is the life of care, which originates from Feminist ethics, and is most commonly called "care ethics." Over the past several decades, it's become one of the most prominent ethical theories, and provides one of the most thoughtful and thorough criticisms of contemporary Western ethics. To briefly sum, care ethics is defined by its focus on promoting positive caring relationships, in light of the emotions and beliefs that result from our interpersonal relationships and our contextual needs in everyday life.

Virginia Held is one of the most prominent care ethicists, and argues that care ethics requires a relational understanding of reality where individuals exist in relation to each other, an inclusion of non-paradigmatic groups like minorities, the mentally ill, and the physically disabled, and that ethics is particularistic, contextual, interactive, and recognizes the role of emotions in the good life. Authors like J.J. Sylvia, in *Doctor Who and Philosophy*'s "Doctor, Who Cares?" have even suggested the Doctor might in fact be a care ethicist. The Doctor's actions in "The Time of the Doctor," and all other episodes where he puts his friends needs above his own and "the greater good," suggests he shares a similar position to care ethics. However, I'd like to suggest that his ethic goes beyond the conceptual grounding of care ethics, which means it isn't quite adequate for our purposes.

As Elizabeth Kiss notes, one of the greatest strengths of care ethics is that it challenges us to see the suffering of particular people in our everyday life. It helps create "real" justice, not some abstract form of justice that is blindly carried out by a good Judoon. As Held muses, care ethics is wonderful at bringing attention to instances of injustice, but it lacks a strong theoretical tool for preventing such injustices from continuing to occur. She suggests the use of rights (and rights-talk), as valuable tools in protecting individuals from the harms of others and structural inequalities. In *The Ethics of Care*, she says, "When rights are viewed in the context of social practices rather than in the abstract, they can effectively express the aspirations of a social movement and 'articulate new values and political vision'." Like Held, I feel we're on the right track, but we need something stronger to ground the Doctor's ethic. So, taking our cue from Held, let's look at one final moral theory, one that uses a theory of rights to respect the contextualized and relational nuances of care ethics. It's here where many of the things we've already discussed will come together to illustrate that Doctor's ethic.

A Life of Needs

In a set of recent books on justice, Nicholas Wolterstorff formulates an intriguing argument for a morality based on peace. The sort of peace that Wolterstorff discusses is not a state of tranquility where nothing bad happens, but instead, it's a state of peace where individuals are engaged in the world, learning about one's own and others' needs, while always striving to ensure all needs are met. In order for people's needs to be met, we all must work and challenge ourselves to not settle for tranquility but to strive for engagement. Being ethical, then, is about justice, a state of affairs where individuals get what they need, or what some would say, deserve. When individuals have their basic needs met, and help provide for the basic needs of others, a state of peace is created. Wolterstorff calls this life of peace 'eirenéism', which is a concept grounded in the Ancient Hebrew concept of shalom—where the universe is in its right place, and everyone within it has their *needs* provided. Instead of using 'eirenéism', I'll simply refer to it as the life of needs.

The life of needs is a life of respecting the rights of others and having one's own rights respected, which culminates in a just state of affairs. Such a morality is intrinsically social, meaning it's based on social relationships, and so, the good-life is intrinsically social too. Once we recognize this social dimension, we see that we're vulnerable to having our rights disrespected, just as others are vulnerable to us. However, with this recognition, we're better-prepared to live a just life that results in our own personal flourishing and others' flourishing, because we recognize these vulnerabilities and live appropriately.

Unlike the virtue ethicist who distances himself from being too emotionally involved with others and things like life, health, pleasure, friends, family, love, beauty, strength, good reputation, and wealth, out of fear of not being happy; the needs ethicist embraces the uncertainties of life. Instead of denying such "natural preferables," they see these preferables as necessary components of being human, and vital to a person's flourishing. They accept the fact that these preferables might be taken away, and that they are highly vulnerable to them being taken away by others. It's the balance between respecting others' rights to their preferables and having our rights respected that comprises the good life. I don't see any way of denying that this is the type of life that the Doctor shows us we should live.

The Doctor's Support

The best way to judge the Doctor's ethic is to watch every episode and read every book since 1963. Realizing not everyone has that sort of time, and that I promised to explain the Doctor's ethic, let me provide a few examples to support the Doctor's life of needs, and then examine a couple of problematic issues.

The best place to start is with the Doctor's willingness to interfere, but since Chapter 3 is dedicated to that sole topic, I'll start by examining the Doctor's compassion. Remember, compassion requires taking on unnecessary suffering, in order to see that others' needs are met. We see the Doctor suffer unnecessarily on several occasions. Take, for instance, the episode "Planet of the Ood" (2008). Donna and the Doctor visit the planet of the Ood, where they discover a mass breading farm for Ood slaves. Through the process of their investigation, the Doctor reveals he can hear the "song" of the Ood—their tortured minds calling out for help, which he shares with Donna. He could've easily done some jiggery pokery with his sonic screwdriver and probably blocked it out, but instead, he chose to listen and suffer along with the Ood. He doesn't need this suffering to know the Ood are being mistreated, or that he should save them; but he takes on their suffering as a compassionate person. He shares their plight and pain, and with great effort he helps release the Ood from their captivity. As a benefit to helping the Ood flourish, he gets to share in their flourishing by hearing their new "song" of joy.

The Doctor's awareness of others' pain is a continual theme in the New Series. In "The Parting of the Ways" (2005), the Doctor claims he can hear "the sun and the moon, the day and the night...all there is, all there was, all there ever could be." He hears how they hurt, and it almost drives him mad. Other Time Lords don't appear to be afflicted with this suffering, yet the Doctor seems to embrace the pain and awareness that it creates. If the Doctor were trying to live the virtuous life or a life of pleasure, he wouldn't continually subject himself to such torment. If he were simply concerned with following rational duties, he wouldn't be concerned with inanimate objects like "the sun and the moon, day and night." What he illustrates over and over is a willingness to consider and seek out those who are in pain, and when he finds them, he acts in ways to bring about a just state of affairs where such things can live in peace.

One might try to chalk the Doctor's actions up to being a hero, not to being compassionate, and in certain cases they're correct. A case can be made that the Doctor is merely a hero in "The Caves of Androzani," when he cures Peri's spectrox toxaemia without saving himself. He might have felt compassion, but according to this argument, we shouldn't call it an act of compassion, since the suffering he takes on was necessary to save Peri's life. The hallmark of compassion is the taking on of unnecessary suffering, and most often, heroes act in cases where the only option is to act. We should be willing to admit that not all of the Doctor's actions are compassionate. It's probably impossible to be totally compassionate every second of the day. However, just a cursory glance of the Doctor's adventures shows he regularly takes on unnecessary suffering. I could spend several chapters listing and describing all of the times the Doctor has risked his life and taken on unnecessary pain and suffering in order to save some "backwoods, no name, hole in the universe" planet from destruction, but I'll let you have the pleasure of exploring those episodes and books.

The point is: If the Doctor thought the good life was anything other than a life of active engagement in the process of seeing that others' needs are met, and peace and justice achieved, then his whole life is a complete and jumbled mess. So, unless we're willing to say he's literally a *madman* with a box or that his actions are based on ignorance or weakness of the will, we should conclude that his concept of the good life best-aligns with some form of the life of needs.

Not so fast! A good critical thinker knows you can't prove a theory merely by finding examples that verify your conclusion. What you need is for your conclusion to stand up to difficult cases. There's no more difficult case, in terms of compassion, than two part serial "Human Nature" and "The Family of Blood" (2007). This story is full of death and destruction, and many claim it could've all been avoided, if the Doctor had gone somewhere else. To top it all, the Doctor condemns the enemies to an "eternity" of suspended animation! How is any of this compassionate?

The serial begins with the Doctor being hunted by "the Family." Because he knows the Family will hunt him forever, the Doctor transforms himself into a human, which by the way, causes him great and unnecessary pain. The Doctor is willing to undergo such pain because if the Family succeeds in stealing his regenerations, they'll spread death throughout the universe forever, and he knows what he'll do to the Family if he stays a Time Lord. His rouse works for a short period of time, but eventually the Family arrives and starts possessing and killing whomever they wish. When events come to a head, the Doctor must make some tough decisions. First, as John Smith, he must decide whether to live a long happy life, married, with a full family, and a peaceful death, or to return to being the Doctor—a lonely alien haunted by the pains of others. The Doctor chooses to forgo his possible life of happiness, and instead stop the Family. This action supports what's been said so far about compassion, however, his punishment of the Family isn't clearly compassionate.

Killing, let alone execution, is not something the Doctor does lightly. Only on rare occasions, like "Runaway Bride" and "Dinosaurs on a Spaceship," do we see the Doctor execute an enemy, and these both occur after the Doctor has been alone for a long period of time. He typically tries to save his adversaries' lives, if he can. So, he decides not to execute the Family. He can't let them go, or they'll simply go back to killing. The only viable options is to grant them their wish for immortality. Some fans see this option as worse than death, but such a conclusion seems too hasty. First off, the Family wants immortality. Like Borusa in "The Five Doctors," this might not be the immortality they envisioned, but it is immortality. Second, we're not privy to the rest of the story. Just as Borusa was eventually freed and allowed to redeem himself in *Engines of War*, it's possible that the Family will one day be released and allowed to redeem themselves.

So, in the end, the most compassionate thing to do is to place the Family where they can't harm others, yet keep them alive in hopes of their redemption. It's obviously a difficult decision for the Doctor, as demonstrated by his annual visits to the little girl, which is a sign of compassion.

The second counterargument one might wage against the Doctor is that he's the bringer of death, the oncoming storm, or some other destructive title. However, the Doctor shouldn't be bothered by these hollow titles. The life of needs requires we accept our vulnerability, and the vulnerability of the universe. It's simply a sad fact that our lives are prone to be damaged by others. Destruction and evil doesn't follow the Doctor, it's always present, whether he's there or not. The reason destruction and evil so often appear around the Doctor is because he refuses to let evil continue with its destructiveness. As Rose said earlier, "The Doctor has the guts to do what is right when everyone else runs away." Sure, you can save yourself by running away or by hiding from evil, but it takes courage to stand up to it. The Doctor could've easily stayed on Gallifrey, watching the universe go by, letting Autons, Cybermen, and Daleks destroy planets, allowing despotic madmen to enslave and kill people, and never let any of this worry him; but he didn't! He decided to take on unnecessary suffering, to risk his life, all in order to ensure that others are able to enjoy their rights to their life-goods. In this way, the Doctor's interference, even when innocents are harmed, promotes the flourishing of all life in the universe.

This Chapter's Cliff-hanger

In the end, the Doctor shows us that in order to flourish as a moral being you must live a life that recognizes your own moral worth and the moral worth of others. Recognizing this moral worth should, then, influence how you treat yourself and others. So far, I've provided a survey discussion of the theoretical grounding for the Doctor's ethics, which serves to ground his way of life. In the next chapter, I'll discuss the more practical application of accepting such an ethic. So, take a break if you need one, and get ready to "get lost."

Notes:

An early version of this paper first appeared as: "Interference, the Doctor, and the Good Life." In *Ruminations, Peregrinations, and Regeneration: A Critical Approach to* Doctor Who. Newcastle upon Tyne, UK: Cambridge Scholars Publishing, 2010. Published with the permission of Cambridge Scholars Publishing.

References:

Episodes:
Doctor Who:
> "The Edge of Destruction" (1963)
> "The Green Death" (1973)
> "Genesis of the Daleks" (1975)
> "The Invisible Enemy" (1977)
> "Robots of Death" (1977)
> "The Invasion of Time" (1978)
> "City of Death" (1979)
> "The Caves of Androzani" (1984)
> "The Parting of the Ways" (2005)

"School Reunion" (2006)
"Runaway Bride" (2006)
"Last of the Time Lords" (2007)
"Planet of the Ood." (2008)
"Journey's End" (2008)
"A Christmas Carol" (2010)
"The Doctor's Wife" (2011)
"Dinosaurs on a Spaceship" (2012)
"Nightmare in Silver" (2013)
"The Time of the Doctor" (2013)

Authors:

Aristotle (1962). *Nicomachean Ethics*. Translated by Martin Ostwald. New Jersey: Prentice Hall; Originally published circa 335-323 BCE.

Bentham, Jeremey. (1988). *The Principles of Moral Legislation*. Amherst, NY: Prometheus Books. Originally published in 1789.

Held, V. (2006). *The Ethics of Care: Personal, Political, and Global*. Oxford: Oxford University Press.

Kant, Immanuel. (1981). *Grounding of the Metaphysics of Morals*, Translated by J. Ellington. Indianapolis, IN: Hackett Publishing. Originally published in 1785.

Kiss, E. (2005). "Justice." In A. M. Jaggar & I. M. Young (Eds.), *Blackwell Companions to Philosophy: A Companion to Feminist Philosophy* (pp. 487–499). Maldan: Blackwell Publishing. Originally published in 1998.

Lewis, Court. (2013). "Understanding Peace Within Contemporary Moral Theory." *Philosophia: Philosophical Quarterly of Israel*. Volume 41, Number 4.

Mann, George. (2013). *Engines of War*. New York: Broadway Books.

Mill, John Stuart. (2002). *Utilitarianism*. Edited by George Sher. Cambridge, MA: Hackett Publishing. Originally published in 1861

Nozick, Robert. (2013). *Anarchy, State and Utopia*. New York: Basic Books. Originally published in 1974.

Sylvia, J.J. (2010). "Doctor, Who Cares?" In *Doctor Who and Philosophy: Bigger on the Inside*, edited by Courtland Lewis and Paula Smithka. Chicago and La

Salle, Illinois: Open Court.

Singer, Peter. (2001). *Writings on an Ethical Life*. New York: Harper Perennial.

Wolterstorff, Nicholas. (2008). *Justice: Rights and Wrongs*. Princeton: Princeton University Press.

Wolterstorff, Nicholas. (2011). *Justice in Love* (Emory University Studies in Law and Religion). Grand Rapids: William B. Eerdmans Publishing.

3

GETTING LOST PROPERLY: THE DOCTOR AS FLÂNEUR

A straight line may be the shortest distance between two points, but it is by no means the most interesting.

—Third Doctor ("Time Warrior," 1973)

Don't worry Ace. It's only a trap!

—Seventh Doctor ("Battlefield," 1989)

You can't just read the guidebook, you've got to throw yourself in! Eat the food, use the wrong verbs, get charged double and end up kissing complete strangers! Or is that just me?

—Ninth Doctor ("The Long Game," 2005)

As seen in the previous chapter, the Doctor shows us that in order to flourish as a moral being you must live a life that recognizes your own moral worth and the moral worth of others. Recognizing this moral worth should, then, influence how you treat yourself and others. However, as is often the case, living the good life is typically easier said than done. Luckily, the Doctor doesn't merely provide us with a theoretical way of structuring our lives and send us alone on our journey. That would be like giving you a key to the TARDIS and saying, "Have fun and don't get into any trouble!" Instead, he invites us to become companions on his journey of being a good moral being. Just like his television companions, we strive and grow from watching the Doctor and encountering the people and places he visits. We've already seen a variety of such lessons, but this chapter describes what appears to be the Doctor's most enduring lesson—how to get lost properly!

Getting lost is probably not what most of you expected, but as the French term 'flâneur' suggests, getting lost provides us with a more direct and intimate interpersonal experience, and it's this sort of interpersonal engagement that's the best way to truly come to understand the symbols and meanings of a people and community. Literally, a flâneur is one who walks around the place she's visiting in order to engage and gain a true understanding of the symbolic meanings and beliefs of the society. Not only does the flâneur gain a deeper understanding of the place she's visiting, but she also gains a better understanding of her own values and needs. If the Doctor's life of need (or, if you prefer, ethic of peace), seen in the previous chapter, is really the best way to structure our lives, then the only way to have peace is to find out what we and others actually need, as opposed to what we "think" they need. The only way to determine the unique emotional, physical, and relational needs of someone else is to get to know them in such a way that we come to have a true understanding of their values, desires, hopes, and dreams. We don't gain this knowledge by remaining distant and separated. We only gain it by getting lost in their world and seeing how they actually perceive and understand the universe. The following pages will examine the Doctor's lessons on how to be a flâneur on *our* world, which is sadly void of sonic screwdrivers and TARDISes.

To Interfere or Not to Interfere

For *Star Trek* fans, the principle of non-interference is as sacred as "love thy neighbor." The "Holy Trek" sums up the principle of non-interference with the "prime directive" (or General Order Number One). As Judith and Garfield Reeves-Stevens describe in their book *Star Trek: Prime Directive*, General Order Number One states:

> The Federation does not allow itself to act as judge and jury to a developing alien culture; Only when cultures have developed to an appropriate point, where they can withstand exposure to an interstellar community, will they be informed of the Federation's existence.

In other words, the prime directive ensures that indigenous alien species don't have their cultures unduly influenced by *Star Fleet* visitors and values.

For *Doctor Who* fans, the prime directive means very little. The Time Lords are the only group that professes to live according to its principles, but as seen in countless episodes, especially from the Third Doctor's tenure, it doesn't take much for them to violate it. According to the Fifth Doctor's comments in "Frontios" (1984), there was once a time when the Time Lords intervened in troublesome situations, but such a policy is part of their distant past. Unlike the non-interference promoted by the prime directive, a principle of *interference* promotes "getting into the thick of things." It allows for accidental visits, crash landings, accidental cultural contaminations, and of course, the purposeful stepping in and saving planets from megalomaniacs and alien invaders.

The difference between interference and non-interference illustrates two ways in which one can engage life. On the one hand, persons practice non-interference by observing life at a safe distance from the comfortable lives and work-environments they've created for themselves. Persons who live according to non-interference take no risks, avoid all possibilities of being embarrassed or being the center of attention, and as a result, never have to face the possibility of failure. On the other hand, persons who practice interference are engaged, take chances, and risk comfort for growth. Granted, there are advantages to the former, like being relatively comfortable and not failing at some task(s), but if you live a life completely disengaged, then you've missed out on what makes living exciting. In fact, if the Doctor's lessons on interference teach us anything, those who do not engage the world around them, in some way, have *failed* at life.

The Virtues of Non-Interference

We shouldn't simply discount non-interference, for it has its own set of virtues. Many anthropological, sociological, and psychological experiments require non-interference to keep data from becoming tainted, either from the responses of the subjects or from the researchers themselves. By not interfering researchers get a more accurate set of data from their study group. What's more, history and global politics provide cases when it's best not to interfere, like when a distant country experiences revolution or civil war. In some instances, interference might be good, but in others, it's best to avoid getting involved. These two examples show that there's a time and place for non-interference.

Furthermore, depending on the nature of reality, non-interference might be the safest approach to ensure we don't "mess up" the universe. For instance, imagine we are time travelers in a semi-*deterministic* universe. In other words, the universe is governed by a strict set of causal laws, but we as humans with free will can act in non-deterministic ways. If this is the nature of reality, then anything we do in the past could destroy the time in which we came and all other future events. So, if determinism is true, then non-interference is truly our best option—assuming the concept of options in a deterministic universe makes sense.

For those unfamiliar with determinism, it is the (deceptively) simple claim that all events have a cause, and these causes are governed by the laws of nature. Since every event is the result of a previous cause, then determinism maintains that the universe is the way it is and can't be otherwise. In other words, the present is determined by a set of specific past events, and the events of the present will create a specific set of future events. The present is determined by the past, and it cannot be otherwise. So, if you were able to go back in time to the distant past and you happened to change one little thing, it would completely alter history as we know it.

We often see this view of reality referred to as the "butterfly-effect," which states that if one travels to the distant past and changes a single thing—in this case, killing a butterfly—the future will be irrevocably changed. Martha Jones states such a position in the 2007 episode "Shakespeare Code":

> **Martha Jones**: But are we safe? I mean, can we move around and stuff?
> **The Doctor**: Of course we can. Why not?
> **Martha Jones**: It's like in those films: if you step on a butterfly, you change the future of the human race.
> **The Doctor**: Then, don't step on any butterflies. What have butterflies ever done to you?

Like Martha in the beginning of her adventures, those who support non-interference typically use the notion of determinism to show why non-interference is the wisest course of action.

One final virtue of non-interference is that it protects observers from being unduly influenced by their research subjects. We might say, observers are to be "affected," not "effected" by their experience. Being influenced—in other words, affected—to some degree can't be helped, but a researcher should never be affected so much that their beliefs and values are changed—what we might call, effected. Such changes could bias the data and taint the results. So, the observer should maintain an objective position in regards to the study group, limiting all interaction that might bias his or her objectivity, which means limiting direct and meaningful contact.

The best examples of this comes from anthropology, sociology, and psychology, where observers study their subjects from a safe distance. They either do not allow their presence to be known, or they limit the awareness of their presence by pretending to be part of the study group. In short, such researchers follow *Star Trek*'s prime directive of non-interference. As seen in many *Star Trek: The Next Generation* episodes and the movie *Insurrection*, members of Star Fleet observe their subjects from a place of safety, and if they have to interact with their subjects, they conceal themselves so as not to allow their presence to become known. This approach is also the goal of the Time Lords, who use their TARDISes to travel, observe, and gather data. In fact, the TARDIS is the ultimate anthropological tool for observing and experimenting on other cultures: it can blend in with any environment, has infinite internal space for gathering and storing samples, a vast array of clothes, and it's connected to the Amplified Panatropic Computer Network linked to the Matrix, which collects and stores all of the Time Lord's and TARDIS's data and experiences for future study.

With the above virtues in mind, the ideal of non-interference is to be an objective observer, and objective observers are *affected* but not *effected* by their subjects. Objective observers are influenced by what they see, but are not changed in the deep and meaningful way people are changed when they engage in intimate personal relationships. The data collection process might change the way the observer acts or thinks, but only in a limited, disconnected way. There's never any "real" interaction between observer and observed, as would occur if a person were to immerse themselves in an environment, take part in its rituals, and interfere with the locals.

Non-interference influences how individuals perceive themselves and how they understand the world around them, and it suggests a way of life that is disengaged and separated from interacting with the world and others. As a result, non-interfering objective observers often miss out on the deep-rooted meanings behind and within the observed society, which also means they add nothing to and gain very little from their experiences.

As we move forward it will become apparent, if it's not already, that *Doctor Who* supports a drastically different understanding of reality and how we should structure our interpersonal lives.

The Virtues of Interference

Being a flâneur requires interference, and there's no set way that a flâneur must understand reality. However, based on our previous discussion of determinism, we can see that reality for the Doctor must allow for some amount of indeterminacy. Indeterminacy can have multiple meanings. For quantum physicists, the universe is indeterminate on a quantum molecular level, and the order we perceive in the world is really the result of random processes. In terms of history, an indeterminate timeline means that cause and effect are such that events in the distant past have little to no effect on the present. Sure, events in the past cause the present, and causes in the near present will affect the world in which we live, but there are no (or very few) determined events—what the Doctor calls "deadlocked"—that must happen in order to create the current state of existence. As a result, our "meddling" with the distant past has little to no effect on the present.

Without going into the details of quantum physics, indeterminacy appears to explain the Doctor's engagement with time. It allows for order in the universe, and it provides a causal explanation of history, but it doesn't create such a strict explanation where killing one butterfly might cause humans to never exist. So, if I go back into the distant past and change something, the present might still occur as it did originally, even though different events caused it. In other words, instead of a linear progression of cause and effect, time is more "wibbly wobbly," and my meddling in the past will neither destroy the fact that I'm writing this sentence on my back porch, nor will it destroy the fabric of the universe. In terms of our historical account, indeterminism would allow for, and benefit from, the existence of deadlocked events. These events would keep history from becoming completely random, and would ensure events "stay on track," even with the Doctor's meddling.

So, instead of worrying over every single action we take while in the past, we can relax, focus on the people we meet, and be more involved in our adventures. The flâneur isn't guided by the concerns of a deterministic universe, where accidentally killing a butterfly— even if the butterfly did nothing to you—might cause the current state-of-affairs to not exist. As a result, you can relax and more-fully enjoy getting lost in their journeys.

In addition to an indeterminate understanding of reality, the flâneur's approach to visiting other cultures is that of a subjective observer—or more precisely a "subjective engager." Flâneurs dive into their environment, change it, and are changed by it. As a result, flâneurs are both *affected* and *effected* by their surroundings. This engagement brings a richness to one's life that is absent from the disengaged objective observer of non-interference. As mentioned above, there's a time and place for non-interference. However, when it comes to our interpersonal subjective lives, being a flâneur not only enriches our lives to a greater extent, but it also enriches the lives of others. When we visit new places and get to know new people, our perception of the world changes, and as result, we change how others perceive the world. Instead of a careful and disconnected engagement with the world and others, being a flâneur calls us to *engage, understand,*

and be *enlightened by* the experience of interference.

The Doctor and Humans as Flâneurs

There's no better flâneur than the Doctor. The earliest account we have of the Doctor is him rejecting the Time Lord's policy of non-interference, in order to be a "rogue." As a result, he's perfectly willing to interfere in *any* situation that he deems worthy of being interfered with. Because of his attitude of interference, the Doctor has saved the universe, saved Earth, and as this book suggests, shown countless real and fictional people a better way to live. For the Doctor, interference is what makes life interesting and exciting. It influences and changes his beliefs and character, while at the same time influencing the beliefs and character of the society he engages. These aspects of interference exemplify what it means to be a flâneur.

To live as a flâneur, however, we must first recognize our own worth and the worth of others. Too often, we see ourselves as unimportant, and we think that the only people of importance are the very few wealthy, popular, and powerful people of the world. According to the Doctor, *no one* is insignificant. As he says in 2010's "A Christmas Carol," "You know that in nine hundred years of time and space and I've never met anybody who wasn't important before." The Doctor is right, but it's up to each of us to recognize the importance of every moment, event, and person we encounter. The best way to do this is by being a flâneur. When you begin living an engaged life, you begin making a difference in others' lives, and they begin making a difference in yours. Once you begin to see your influence on others, your community, and the world, you begin to see why the Doctor has never met anyone who wasn't important.

Maybe you think you're not important—but you are! You have near-infinite potential to learn and grow, to influence and change the lives of others, and to make the universe a better place. We're all *affected* and *effected* by the people and places we engage, which means we're surrounded by opportunities to engage and to be engaged. Though we often focus on a small number of "great" historical figures, *history is made by everyone who's brave enough to engage and interfere with the world in which they're lucky enough to live*. By engaging the world we make history. When we don't interfere, we passively become part of it. If we ignore the part we play in making history, then not only do we forget how important we are, but the whole universe loses some of its character. The Doctor challenges us to step out of our comfort zones and embrace getting lost.

No matter our abilities, weaknesses, or skill-sets, we can all be flâneurs. Not everyone has a TARDIS, a sonic screwdriver, or 12-ish regenerations. Yet, we all have the power to choose to be more engaged and more willing to leave our comfort zones in order to be more like a flâneur. One such approach to getting lost is to use film, television, and books. Good entertainment not only offers a spectacle, but it also offers individuals the opportunity to visit a variety of times and places, share a multitude of experiences with many diverse people and cultures, and to grow from the experience.

For some people, shows like *Doctor Who* take the place of lost friends and family, or they provide an opportunity to travel, which is beyond their physical and/or economic means. Really good fiction mirrors what happens to Jean Luc Picard in the *Star Trek: The Next Generation* episode "The Inner Light," where Picard lives a life's worth of experiences—including making friends, falling in love, and having kids—in the matter of 30 minutes. Furthermore, writers like Harry Middleton suggest a similar type of travel based merely on one's ability to imagine. In the *Earth is Enough*, Middleton talks of his two uncles who, with the aid of an atlas, travel to different places and times, in order to see parts of the world they know they'll never have the opportunity to visit. Like all current attempts at time travel, this "time travel" is the result of the imagination, but it still serves to illustrate that we can be engaged flâneurs from the comfort of our homes, as long as when we engage others—whether in person, via the Internet, or by some other means—we apply the lessons we've learned.

Joining the Journey

Look at what happens in the very first serial of *Doctor Who*, "An Unearthly Child" (1963). The Doctor ends up abducting two school teachers and taking them all over time and space. Not only do Barbara and Ian begin a fantastic journey that challenges every preconceived notion they've ever held, but it begins our journey of rethinking everything we thought we knew. From every adventure, companion, world, enemy, and narrow escape we grow and learn more about what it means to be a good person.

We're to learn to seek out and embrace the unexpected. When we visit a place we must not settle for what's on the tour map or for what everyone else is doing. Instead, we need to seek out the things so intimately tied to a place's essence that they are often overlooked by everyone else. Venturing out allows us to find lesser-known places that are full of excitement and mystery, "unknown" treasures that will change the way we understand the world, wise sages that challenge the reality of who we are, a forgotten hero memorialized in a statue, a beautiful sunset, a nearly-erased historical tale, a forgotten gravesite, and who knows what else?! It's this type of engagement that shapes who we are and how we understand the world around us, while at the same time enriching the places we visit. This is what being an interfering flâneur is like, and this is what the Doctor teaches us to do.

As often noted by vacationers, the most strenuous and challenging vacations are usually the most enjoyable and refreshing. Such vacations invite us to step outside of our comfort zones, loosen up, and get involved in things that we would have never thought possible. Just like when the Doctor takes viewers to places beyond their imagination, traveling as a flâneur challenges us to change who we are for the better. And because of this, we should all live our lives as flâneurs—no matter the time and space we exist.

References:

Episodes:
Doctor Who
"An Unearthly Child" (1963)
"Time Warrior" (1973)
"Frontios" (1984)
"Battlefield" (1989)
"Shakespeare Code" (2007)
"A Christmas Carol" (2010)

Star Trek: The Next Generation
"Who Watches the Watchers" (1989)
"The Inner Light" (1992)

Star Trek: Insurrection

Authors:
Middleton, Harry. *The Earth is Enough: Growing up in a World of Flyfishing, Trout, and Old Men* (Boulder, CO: Pruett Publishing Company, 1989).

Reeves-Stevens, Judith and Garfield. *Star Trek: Prime Directive*. New York: Pocket Books, 1990.

CHAPTER 4

AVOIDING MONSTERS: STUDIES IN EVIL

> There are some corners of the universe which have bred the most terrible things. Things which act against everything that we believe in. They must be fought.
>
> —Second Doctor ("The Moonbase," 1967)

I've spent a lot of time talking about how and why to do good things, but how do we avoid becoming monsters? More specifically, what character traits and behaviors are immoral, how do we recognize them, and how do we avoid allowing them to turn us into monsters? Answering these questions, or at least shedding some light on them, is the goal of this chapter. Before we can start, however, we need to clarify what we're talking about when we say 'monster'.

'Monster' is a word that gets thrown around a lot. We have legendary monsters like Dracula, Big Foot, and Loch Ness. We have what some people might call "pop culture monsters," like Kanye West, "Tot Mom," Nancy Grace, and (insert your most-hated pop culture figure here). Finally, of course, we have moral monsters like Adolf Hitler, Joseph Stalin, and Charles Manson. Are all of these "monsters?" If they are, then it's safe to assume that the term 'monster' is being used in different ways. The first group are monsters because they are creatures, strangely alien and otherworldly. The second group are "monsters" because we don't like the way they act. We've vilified them to such a degree that they seem to be different than the rest of society's "normal" folk, so we call them monsters. The last group are monsters because they chose to participate and delight in the killing of innocent people, with no hint of regret or remorse.

It's this last group of moral monsters that will be the focus of this chapter. We can learn a lot about how not to act by looking at legendary and pop culture monsters, and we'd see that both share some basic character traits. My goal, however, is to examine moral monsters from *Doctor Who*, in order to provide some general observations about the lessons *Doctor Who* teaches us about how *not* to act, which will then better-help us live the good life.

We must begin by recognizing that we often do ourselves a disservice when we call our fellow humans monsters. Doing so not only dehumanizes, but it also fictionalizes the person or thing we call "monster." Why might this be bad? Well, if we're to learn anything from these "monsters," we need them to be like us. In other words, since we're human, we need them to be human. If we're not careful, calling a person a "monster" can turn them into something non-human, something different, strange, and alien. They become something distant, an anomaly, something we don't have to worry about becoming because we're human, not monsters. Take Hitler for instance: if he's turned into a non-human monster, then the Holocaust becomes a terrible fluke of history, one of which we never have to worry about happening again; nor do we have to worry about "us" ever participating in the mass-extermination of innocents because we're "normal" humans that would never mass-exterminate innocents. As Jonathan Glover's *Humanity* disturbingly illustrates, such an intellectual position is false. Hitler was *all-too-human*, and just like all the people who helped Hitler achieve his goals, all of "us" good "normal" humans are just as *capable* of holding similar beliefs and acting in similar ways, whether we're willing to admit it or not.

Over the past fifty years *Doctor Who* has given us a plethora of monsters, ranging from the ludicrous—but quite tasty—Kandyman ("The Happiness Patrol," 1988) to the mundane, like human collaborators such as Luke Rattigan ("The Sontaran Stratagem" and "The Poison Sky," 2008). In between these extremes, viewers have faced Daleks, Cybermen, Zygons, Vashta Nerada, Weeping Angels, and among many others, Silents. Each one of *Doctor Who*'s monsters provides a fictional caricature of what it means for humans to be monsters. As Graham Sleight nicely illustrates in the book *The Doctor's Monsters*, each one exhibits a "narrowness" of behavior that is in tension with the Doctor's "flexibility." I think Sleight is correct in his analysis, and I would recommend his book for anyone truly interested in the nature of *Doctor Who*'s monsters, but I will take a different approach to examining the monsters of *Doctor Who*, since being a moral monster has nothing to do with appearance.

Doctor Who typically associates being a monster with a person's evil motives and desires, so this is the approach taken below. So, to understand *Doctor Who*'s monsters, we need to understand evil, and to make sense of both, we'll examine some of *Doctor Who*'s most famous monsters. From these studies, we'll learn the Doctor's lesson on how to avoid becoming a monster in our own lives.

What Makes A Monster?

To be a moral monster a person must carry out acts that we might call evil. 'Monster' implies a spectrum of wrongdoing. If all wrongdoing is monstrous, then the word 'monster' is meaningless, for it only means 'immoral', and if it only means 'immoral', then we're all monsters. There are certain Eastern and Western religious traditions that hold humans are naturally evil, which supports such a conclusion. Does the Doctor think humans are naturally evil?

As we've seen in previous chapters, the Doctor rejects the idea that humans are naturally evil. He even goes so far as to believe that Daleks are redeemable ("Into the Dalek," 2014). The Doctor seems to agree with Laurence Thomas's conclusion that humans aren't naturally evil, though they can be easily motivated to both perform evil acts and to allow evil acts to occur. In *Vessels of Evil*, Thomas discusses American slavery and the Holocaust, and points to psychological studies like Philip Zimbardo's Stanford Prison Experiments and Stanley Milgram's experiments on the obedience to authority, to show how evil is perpetrated by ordinary fragile human beings. It's our fragility, discussed in-depth in Chapter 2, which is often the root of our fears and feelings of inadequacy and hatred, and it's what makes us so susceptible to not only allow evil to flourish but also to actively participate in evil. What often occurs is we strive to do what we feel to be right, but if we're not careful we can become morally sullied. Like an outfit that gets dirty and dingy over time, our moral character can become tainted; so much so that we can even find ourselves delighting in harmful acts. When we reach the point of delighting in harmful acts, we've become evil—what I refer to as a moral monster.

Based on this cursory understanding of what it means to be a moral monster, we can't say a thing is a monster simply by the way it looks. The Eleventh Doctor episode "Hide" (2013) provides us with a scary monster who not only haunts a mansion, but also haunts a different time zone. Viewers spend the entire episode fearing the "monster," which in the end, is nothing more than an alien creature trying to reunite with its long lost love. Sadly, Neil Cross chose to focus on the (rather mundane) human story instead of exploring the monster's story—a story of two monstrously hideous creatures who cause no direct harm and are motivated only by a desire to be reunited with their one true love, yet are feared and hunted by humans. It might be part of humanity's common language to label the Crooked Man a "monster," but in terms of morality, it's a misuse of the word 'monster'. It's biased and offensive. It redefines 'monster' as 'ugly', and is no different than calling someone with a mental or physical defect a monster. If 'monster' is to have any moral weight, it must mean more than just 'ugly'. The concept of monster, then, must include some sort of evil or despicable behavior that is inconsistent with human morality.

There are fairly uncontroversial instances of evil—though as you might guess, when it comes to morality nothing is completely uncontroversial. Such evils include mass atrocities like genocide, rape camps, torture, and the indiscriminate killing of innocents. There are also more controversial instances of evil: violence in general, which includes war and capital punishment, manipulation, wickedness, and for some, anything that prevents a person's natural flourishing, which would including telling lies. To make things easy, and to get a glimpse of why there's disagreement over what is evil, let's make a helpful distinction between *quantitative* and *qualitative* evil. Quantitative evil maintains that an act like killing might be bad because it causes pain, or wrong because it violates a person's rights, but it isn't evil in itself. It only becomes evil when a certain quantity of people are killed. So, a Slitheen killing the Prime Minister of the United Kingdom is bad, but they didn't become evil until they started killing multiple people. With quantitative evil, it's all about the numbers. Of course, one of the difficulties of quantitative evil is answering the question: "At what point does it become evil?" If we say a Dalek killing one human isn't evil, but a Dalek killing a thousand humans is evil; then, at what point did it become evil? Whatever number we choose appears random, since there appears to be no qualitative difference between any of the numbers. If 789 is the magic number, then what happens between it and 788 to make it evil? Nothing appears to have happened, except one more person has been murdered.

If there's no difference, then quantitative evil appears to be a hollow concept. So, instead of looking at the numbers, some see evil as a qualitative concept. Evil, then, is about the type of action performed, or the motives behind an action. The difference between 'murder' and 'kill' is a good illustration. By definition, murder is unjustified killing. In terms of the law, 'unjustified' means it breaks the law, but we're interested in morality, not legality. So, in terms of morality, 'unjustified' means there's no moral justification for such an act. What's an example of justified killing? Self-defense is the most common example. If someone attacks you, and during your defense you inadvertently kill him, most ethicists (even many pacifists) will say your act is morally justified. It's this principle of self-defense that often grounds other arguments that involve killing: war, capital punishment, abortion, etc. When killing is unjustified, for whatever reason, it's considered murder, and if a person believes certain acts are evil, murder is one of the most obvious examples.

The proponent of qualitative evil maintains that something qualitatively different happens when a person commits certain acts. Using our Slitheen example from above, the Slitheen commit an evil act as soon as they murder another person. They didn't care that the Prime Minister was an autonomous person with a life and dreams. They only cared about themselves and their selfish desire to murder and sell the planet for profit. The Daleks, too, are evil because they go around enslaving and murdering people. In Trevor Baxendale's book *Prisoner of the Daleks*, the Daleks even calculate how to cause the most pain for the longest amount of time with their guns—evil indeed! So, not only do they murder, but they delight in the pain and suffering of creatures while they're dying. The Daleks' motives and delight in murdering are why they're so reviled by the Doctor as evil.

The distinction between quantitative and qualitative evil gives us a better understanding of what we should consider evil. Quantitative evil is an intuitively plausible concept, but it doesn't shed much light on why a person is evil. It's probably best just to admit that evil has a certain magnitude of wrongdoing, coupled with the intent of a wrongdoer, and avoid trying to pinpoint a specific number associated with when something becomes evil. Qualitative evil, and its ability to bring motivational desires into the discussion of immoral acts like murder, provides a stronger basis on which to make sense of evil and why some of *Doctor Who*'s villains are appropriately titled monsters.

A Silver Nemesis's Motives

One of my favorite "monsters" of *Doctor Who* is the Cybermen. In *Doctor Who and Philosophy: Bigger on the Inside*, I argue that the Cybermen aren't evil. Bonnie Green and Chris Willmott refer to my defense as the "altruistic interpretation" in their chapter "The Cybermen as Human.2," featured in *New Dimensions of Doctor Who*. I admit I tend to be overly sympathetic when it comes to the Cybermen, but if it's true that they have no emotions (leaving aside those annoying instances of writers giving them emotions for dramatic effect), then it seems impossible for them to be evil. I wholeheartedly agree that their willingness to harm and destroy creates extremely bad consequences, in the sense that it produces a lot of pain and suffering. However, they have no emotions, and so make no self-directed autonomous decisions or actions. As a result, they're more akin to a force of nature, which lacks any sort of intent or motive, than a monster.

It's true that Cybermen do a lot of really bad things, like persistently "upgrading" humans and killing anything and everything else that doesn't serve their purely logical interests. However, just because a thing performs bad actions, it doesn't necessarily mean that it's evil or it's done evil. The two moral theories of utilitarianism and duty ethics help us see how this is possible, because they make clear the difference between causing pain vs. doing wrong. Lots of things cause pain in life, but pain in itself isn't wrong. If it were, going to the dentist, going to school, and growing older, which all involve pain, would be wrong. For utilitarianism, what's important is that we perform actions or follow moral rules that create a balance of pleasure over pain, where pleasure is maximized as much as possible. So, for utilitarians, pain is bad, but it's not wrong.

For duty ethicists, pain has no moral standing. Morally motivated actions are either right or wrong. With duty ethics, then, we might have actions that are bad (they cause pain), but are morally right (they follow some moral principle); and we might have actions that are good (they cause pleasure), but are morally wrong (they violate a moral principle). With these distinctions the Cybermen should be understood as creating lots of bad, but due to their lack of autonomously generated motives, they shouldn't be understood as being evil. Crazy, right?! Not really. It's only crazy if you think natural disasters like hurricanes, volcanos, and tornadoes are evil. Let's examine motives more closely and see why natural disasters and Cybermen aren't evil.

A Cyber-Natural Disaster

Actions are based on our desires, and desires are what motivate action. One of the oldest theories of human action is "psychological egoism," which claims humans can only perform actions that are in their own self-interests. This theory is easy to verify. By performing an action, you've done what you wanted to do. Even if a Cyberman holds a gun to you and says, "Tell me where the Doctor is, or you will be deleted," it's your choice whether to talk or to remain silent. Your decision illustrates what you understand to be in your best interests. As we've seen before, verification doesn't prove something true, so we can't say with certainty that psychological egoism is true. Nevertheless, psychological egoism is intuitively plausible and remains a prominent psychological explanation for what motivates human action.

If we assume psychological egoism is true, it still doesn't explain moral motives. Psychological egoism simply describes human psychology, and remember, ethics is concerned with how the world should be, not how the world is. Since humans have the freedom to choose (volition) how we act, even if we're driven by the motive to do what's in our own best interests, we can make complex moral decisions that conflict with our best interests. For instance, if you remain silent when the Cyberman asks you the location of the Doctor, then you're putting the life of the Doctor and his interests over your own life. As a result, even though you're choosing to do what you want to do, which supports psychological egoism, your value system motivates you to do what's best for the Doctor—and whoever else he happens to be saving at the time.

This other-centered approach is called altruism. Altruists consider the desires and needs of others and act in such a way to make sure their needs are met; indeed, sometimes at the expense of one's own desires and needs. I've already argued that the Doctor operates on a similar moral principle, but counter to my argument in *Doctor Who and Philosophy*, it's impossible for the Cybermen to be altruists, or any other sort of egoist. In fact, if what we know about the Cybermen is true, that they lack any sort of emotions, then they can't make any sort of volitional acts independent of their "programming." Except for maybe the Cyber Controller/Leader, most Cybermen act as mere automatons, so they seem no different than a poorly programmed computer. If they had desires and the emotional states that ground desires, then we could fault them for not trying to be better, or to correct their programming flaws. Since they lack such desires and emotions, then it'd be wrong to call them evil.

Evil requires volition, and one of the best accounts of volition comes from David Hume. In *A Treatise of Human Nature*, Hume argues that human action isn't motivated by reason alone—a pretty radical idea at the time. Since at least the time of Socrates, reason was thought to be the mechanism behind human action. Hume argues, instead, that intentional actions come from passions. These passions are most often simply the result of instinctual responses to stimuli like pleasure and pain. A cool wind causes me to want a jacket, or the empty feeling in my stomach makes me long for something tasty to eat. A stimulus creates a passion, which creates a desire, which then motivates us to satisfy the desire. Reason plays no role in the creation of desires and motives. For Hume, reason only arises when we set out to satisfy our desires, by helping us reason how best to go about satisfying it.

Without the desire for a jacket or food, we wouldn't seek such things. If we had no desires, then we'd never seek out anything. So, if all we have is logic and reason, and no emotional passions, then we'd never have desires or the motive to seek out anything. We'd be mindless automatons, following some pre-programmed motive, and as a result, we wouldn't be morally autonomous. We'd be more like a force of nature that has no intentions, motives, desires, or any other sort of moral component. Hume's argument is the true weakness of Cybermen, because it shows that if Cybermen are truly motivated by pure logic, free from pain, fear, and for the most part, death ("The Tenth Planet," 1966), then they aren't moral beings. They're simply poorly-programmed machines, and no matter how annoying and dangerous a poorly-programmed machine is, it's wrong to call such a thing evil. If they aren't evil, or even capable of being moral, then they aren't moral monsters.

In the New Series, where Cybermen are created by John Lumic to rid humans of pain and suffering, they lack all human emotions, which means they lack all desires ("The Rise of the Cybermen"/"Age of Steel," 2006). Instead of human emotions responding to stimuli, they are programmed to respond to stimuli. This difference means Cybermen don't voluntarily choose to perform an action; instead, their programming determines what they choose. It's like the difference between you saying: "I chose to watch *Doctor Who*" vs. "My DVR chose to record *Doctor Who*." The former required volition, while the latter simply followed a programmed command.

We can criticize John Lumic and the logicians from the Classic Series for how they programmed the Cybermen, and we can call them moral monsters, but it's a misuse of the term to call Cybermen monsters. They're more like a natural disaster, and though there are some who refer to hurricanes and tornadoes as "natural evils," I would argue—and I think the Doctor would agree—that calling such things "evil" is wrong, especially since we always find the Doctor fighting against the monster causing the natural disaster, not the disaster itself ("Enemy of the World," 1968 and "The Fires of Pompeii," 2008); unless he knows of a way of preventing it. Even then, he's fighting to save people's lives, not fighting against the disaster.

Dalek Hatred

The Daleks and Cybermen share many similarities, but they're markedly different. No, not because it only takes three Daleks to wipe out a Cyberarmy, but because the Daleks have emotions. Granted, they only have a set of limited emotions, and depending on the needs of story, they're sometimes portrayed as being as mindless and logical as Cybermen. The majority of Dalek lore, however, shows that they are driven by the emotions of hatred and superiority. No matter how limited, these are emotions, and so it's appropriate to call Daleks both evil and monstrous.

Hatred in itself isn't evil. I hate seeing young children starved, mistreated, and abused. When I see such things my hatred of them motivates me to stand up and act, to help those in need. This is exactly what the Doctor does in "The Beast Below" (2010), when he reveals he can't stand off to the side and do nothing when he hears a child cry. So, what makes hatred evil?

The answer isn't easy. Hatred typically clouds the mind and prevents clear rational thought. It makes us do rash things, like summarily judging and killing evil despots like Solomon ("Dinosaurs on a Spaceship," 2012), which is contrary to the "way we roll" ("A Town Called Mercy," 2012). Hatred can also focus the mind, so much so that our vision becomes myopic—we focus on one thing while ignoring everything around us. When our vision becomes myopic, we often become willfully blind to the harms and wrongdoings we commit. We see this happen when species like the Zygons, Silurians, and the Saturnyns from "Vampires of Venice" (2010) are driven to destroy other species by the hatred of their possible extinction. Their hatred, then, causes them to not only destroy innocent lives and the moral principles of justice that might ground their society, but to cause their own destruction in the process.

The Daleks, however, exhibit a different sort of hatred. Their hatred, often considered analogous of Nazism, is a hatred of all things impure and different from themselves. Jonathan Glover examines the moral history of the 20th Century in *Humanity*, and he attributes much of the evil of the century to "tribalism" and closed "belief systems." Tribalism manifests itself in a "us vs. them" mentality, which turns "them"—the Other—into something dangerous—a disease, a cancer, and mortal threat. Closed belief systems, sometimes simply referred to as ideologies, are marked by a controlled set of beliefs that cares little for truth and allows no dissension. Closed belief systems are the hallmark of fundamentalist religious groups who reject facts and reason and are willing to harm and kill those who disagree, fundamentalist racist regimes like the Nazis and the Ku Klux Klan, and ideological regimes like communist Russia and Maoist China. Glover provides several wonderful examples of closed belief systems. In Stalinist Russia, instead of letting the facts guide their study of genetics, Stalin rejected Mendelian genetics in favor of Lamarckian genetics, since the latter seemed more "Marxist." Based on Lamarckian genetics, Stalin claimed to be able to turn apple trees into orange trees—sometimes truth is stranger than fiction. Since scientists could be exiled or killed for dissenting, they focused all of their research and farming resources on Lamarckian genetics. As a result, crops failed and people starved and died. In Maoist China, logic professors were persecuted for teaching principles like validity, which held people to an objective standard of truth and showed Maoist positions to be inconsistent.

The Daleks' evil and monstrousness is grounded in tribalism and a closed belief system. Their tribe is the Daleks, and if anyone is even slightly different, they are both inferior and unworthy of shared existence. Even fellow "Daleks" run the risk of becoming too different, as seen in "Evolution of the Daleks" (2007), "Victory of the Daleks" (2010), and the oft-referred to Dalek civil war ("Remembrance of the Daleks," 1988). Davros isn't even immune from the hatred of the Daleks ("Genesis of the Daleks," 1975 and "Resurrection of the Daleks," 1984). Their tribalism reinforces their belief system of hatred and domination that sees the universe as belonging to the Daleks, to be used as they see fit.

Dalek tribalism and their belief system is only possible if they have some sort of emotion that motivates action. Even though they lack emotions like compassion and concepts like friendship, they're capable of transcending their natural tendencies. Humans share many Dalek tendencies and motives, but most of us choose not to act upon them in our daily lives. Granted, for dramatic effect, the writers often present the Daleks as lacking a "human perspective" ("The Evil of the Daleks," 1967 and "Evolution of the Daleks), but from the history of the Daleks we don't see on TV, the Daleks continuously make complex decisions about how to live their lives and structure society. We could say it's in their nature and so they can't do anything about it. If we take this approach, then there's no morality—the worst possible conclusion, since all natural desires (killing, raping, abusing, etc.) would be morally acceptable. We should, instead, understand the Daleks as being capable of growing and learning from their complex emotional desires, no matter how limited they are in relation to humans. Like humans, they might choose not to overcome their base-desires, but that makes them even more responsible for their wrongdoing. For audiences, then, the lesson to be learned is that when we dogmatically believe in a closed belief system, and we see our "tribe"—whether it's our community, country, religion, or species—as the only valuable one, we exhibit Dalek tendencies of being evil moral monsters. We should instead strive to overcome our natural desires to do wrong, and to stand by while wrongdoing occurs, and instead strive to live morally engaged lives.

The Evil of Manipulation

Being a monster doesn't require you to go around killing a bunch of innocent people. In fact, our typical human monsters never kill anyone. Did Hitler ever actually kill anyone during his leadership of the NAZIs? No, but he ordered and is responsible for the death of millions. Bernie Madoff destroyed people's lives, and some of these people committed suicide, but he never murdered anyone. Parents around the globe abuse their children, both physically and mentally. Some even sell their children into prostitution and slavery. Spouses manipulate and abuse each other, and among many other instances of evil, some corporations knowingly enslave, poison, and kill innocent people, usually the ones making and using their products. Where is this sort of evil in *Doctor Who*?

Like real life, these sorts of evil are simply woven into the fabric of the show. We see it occur when the Ood are enslaved ("Plant of the Ood," 2008). The Nestene Consciousness often materializes as part of a broader corporation ("Spearhead from Space," 1970). Children are often harmed and manipulated (Arguably, all of Amy Pond's episodes are the result of her being manipulated, 2010-2012). I could spend a book just talking about these "everyday" evils. Instead, let's focus on one particular type of evil that is arguably one of the most common human evils: manipulation. Of course, if we're going to talk about manipulation, then there's no greater example of manipulation than the Master/Missy. From his devious machinations with the Axons ("The Claws of Axos," 1971) to her attempt to make the Doctor the "President" of the universe ("Dark Water/Death in Heaven," 2014), the Master presents us with a very human monster—a person who lies and deceives to get everything s/he wants.

You might be saying, "You're kidding, right. I'm nothing like the Master/Missy." Think about every time you've wanted something, and in order to get it, you've told a lie. I couldn't turn in my paper because my grandmother died. I was speeding because I had to get some place really important, or simply, I wasn't speeding. I don't feel good and can't come into work today. I don't have any change. I think you look great. I don't know how that got there!

Why is it so easy and natural to lie? As we see on "The Time of the Doctor" (2013), even the Doctor struggles with telling the truth. The good news is that just because you lie, it doesn't mean you're a monster. Telling lies, however, can morph you into a monster, because lying is a form of disrespect and manipulation. It helps us get what we want without facing the possible dangers of telling the truth. The Master, then, gives us a nice illustration of the type of monster we resemble when we make lying and manipulation a habit. Of course, most of us won't go around trying to conquer the world with our lies, but lying and manipulation is an attempt to conquer our own little world. If we go around trying to conquer through lying and manipulation, we'll become our own version of the Master/Missy. However, if we go around conquering the world through compassion and understanding, we'll become our own version of the Doctor.

Where Do We Go From Here?

As Friedrich Nietzsche suggests in *The Will to Power*, much of life involves us trying to shape the world according to our will. It's up to us to choose how we go about shaping the world. You can shape it by being evil and manipulative, or by being persistent and compassionate. Regardless of how you engage the world, it's up to you to decide if your passions are moral, and whether or not you're going to act upon them. Of course, there are exceptions to the rule, for some cognitive disorders prevent fully-volitional acts. In such cases we should help, or provide the help needed that will allow such individuals to flourish in their own way.

We're greater than Cybermen because we have the will to choose how to act. Sometimes we resemble Daleks with our close-minded tribalism, but no matter how limited our emotional states, we can always rise above our natural tendencies—at least that's what the Doctor teaches. Just like Daleks, we can sometimes resemble many of the moral monsters on *Doctor Who*. The monsters on *Doctor Who* provide us with a reflection of ourselves, and if we pay attention, we can learn how to change ourselves from being monsters to being heroes.

References:
Episodes:
Doctor Who
    "The Tenth Planet" (1966)
    "The Moonbase" (1967)
    "Evil of the Daleks" (1967)
    "Enemy of the World" (1968)
    "Spearhead from Space" (1970)
    "The Claws of Axos" (1971)
    "Genesis of the Daleks" (1975)
    "Resurrection of the Daleks" (1984)
    "Remembrance of the Daleks" (1988)
    "The Happiness Patrol" (1988)
    "The Rise of the Cybermen" (2006)
    "Age of Steel" (2006)
    "Evolution of the Daleks" (2007)
    "Fires of Pompeii" (2008)
    "Planted of the Ood" (2008)
    "The Poison Sky" (2008)
    "The Sontaran Stratagem" (2008)
    "The Beast Below" (2010)
    "Victory of the Daleks" (2010)
    "The Vampires of Venice" (2010)
    "Dinosaurs on a Spaceship" (2012)
    "A Town Called Mercy" (2012)
    "Hide" (2013)
    "The Time of the Doctor" (2013)
    "Into the Dalek" (2014)
    "Dark Water" (2014)
    "Death in Heaven" (2014)

Authors:

Baxendale, Trevor. (2009). Prisoner of the Daleks. London: Random House UK.

Glover, Jonathan. (2012). *Humanity: A Moral History of the 20th Century*, 2nd edition. New Haven, CT: Yale University Press.

Green, Bonnie and Chris Willmott. (2013). "The Cybermen as Human.2." In *New Dimensions of Doctor Who: Adventures in Space, Time and Television*. Edited by Matt Hills. London: I. B. Tauris.

Hume, David. (2000). *A Treatise of Human Nature*. Edited by David Fate Norton and Mary J. Norton. Oxford: Clarendon Press.

Lewis, Courtland. (2010). "Cybermen Evil, I Don't Think So." In *Doctor Who and Philosophy: Bigger on the Inside*. Edited by Courtland Lewis and Paula Smithka. Chicago and La Salle, Illinois: Open Court.

Milgram, Stanley. (1983). *Obedience to Authority*. New York: Harper Perennial.

Nietzsche, Friedrich. (1968). *The Will to Power*. Edited by Walter Kaufmann. Translated by Walter Kaufmann and R. J. Hollingdale. New York: Vintage Books.

_____. (2000). *Basic Writings of Nietzsche*, Translated by Walter Arnold Kaufmann. New York: Modern Library.

Sleight, Graham. (2012). *The Doctor's Monsters: Meanings of the Monstrous in Doctor Who*. New York: I.B. Tauris.

Thomas, Laurence Mordekhai. (1993). *Vessels of Evil: American Slavery and the Holocaust*. Philadelphia: Temple University Press.

Zimbardo, Philip. (Accessed 2015). "Stanford Prison Experiment." http://www.prisonexp.org/.

5

THE WRATH OF THE DOCTOR

> That is the role you seem determined to play, so it seems that I must play mine! The man that stops the monsters!
>
> —Twelfth Doctor ("Flatline," 2014)

We've already examined many instances of how the Doctor responds to the challenges of life, and I've argued that one of the key features of the Doctor's understanding of the good life is that we must recognize our own vulnerability. By recognizing these vulnerabilities, and the power we have over whether we help or harm others, we begin to see ourselves as part of an inter-connected moral community with all other moral entities. So, instead of being afraid and hiding our vulnerabilities, we should embrace them and engage the world with full-knowledge that we might get hurt in the process; attempting to make the world and ourselves a little better in the process.

However, as the last chapter illustrated, there's evil in the world, and the more we engage, the more we're likely to be harmed and wronged. It's simply a fact of life that by accident, or by careful planning, people wrong each other, and yes, we wrong other people. So, how should we respond to wrongdoing? The justice of punishment, called retributive justice (think retribution), is complex and difficult. How do we determine what a wrongdoer deserves? Is it enough to say, "An eye for an eye?" Is this a limit on what we can do, meaning *no more* than an eye may be taken? Or is it a prescription, saying we must take an eye? If it's the latter, then how do we determine equal punishment? If someone murders your friend, then is the "equal" punishment to murder their friend? That can't be right.

Philosophers of law will often talk about the arbitrariness of laws and punishments. Basically, legislators create a list of crimes ranked in order from bad to worst; then after creating a similar list of punishments, try to match both up. Since there are no laws found in nature that tell us how we should punish, like all murderers should be killed, we must rely on ethics to justify what should happen. Even when we let reason rule over our emotions and passions, determining appropriate moral punishments can seem as arbitrary as determining legal punishments. So, what sort of approach does the Doctor take to punishment?

The Doctor Dances

It's often said, it takes two to tango. Well, except in instances of self-wronging, it also takes at least two to be wronged. You need a perpetrator who wrongs another person, and you need a victim who is the recipient of the wrongdoing. When a wrongdoing occurs both perpetrator and victim deserve something. Morally speaking, the perpetrator deserves blame and/or punishment, while the victim deserves some sort of restitution. In everyday language, we usually say they both deserve justice, and perpetrators and victims both "get justice" when perpetrators are properly punished. When perpetrators aren't properly punished, an injustice occurs.

This sort of language is often too simplistic and obscures the true nature of retributive justice. First off, no one "gets" justice. Justice isn't *the punishment* a wrongdoer gets, nor is it the money a victim receives. It might require such things, but it isn't an object to be given. Justice is a state of affairs (a moral relationship) between people, one that prescribes certain actions be performed after a wrongdoing.

Second, moral and legal justice are two different things, yet we must not ignore that within civil society they're intimately intertwined. If my wife dies as a result of Ms. Gillyflower's despicable plan in "The Crimson Horror" (2013), she's violated my wife's moral and legal rights not to be murdered. As a result of the violation of her legal right, the police should arrest and the courts should punish Ms. Gillyflower. They don't arrest and prosecute her for violating my wife's moral right. If Ms. Gillyflower promised my wife to introduce her to Mr. Sweet, but never did, then she's violated my wife's moral right not to be lied to; but the police aren't going to come and arrest her for such a lie. Civil society is in charge of punishment relating to legal rights, and individuals are in charge of moral punishments. In civil society, the legal and the moral will often overlap, but not always. Let's examine some possible difficulties.

If Ms. Gillyflower slapped my wife, then an appropriate moral punishment might be that my wife gets to slap her back. But if she murders my wife, then my wife has no way of punishing her. The burden falls to my wife's loved ones, like me. I, then, have several options. I can scorn, resent, and among other things, hate Ms. Gillyflower, but in a civil society I'm supposed to let the law determine her punishment and hope that it prevails in quenching my moral outrage. When the legal system works, we call this both legal and moral justice.

As we all know, however, the law doesn't always work. Crooked judges and lawyers, news media, social pressures, ignorance, jury tampering, and among a whole host of other things, common human error can all prevent justice from occurring. Peter French provides an excellent examination of when justice fails in *Cowboy Metaphysics* and *The Virtues of Vengeance*. Especially in the latter, French argues that vengeance is tied to our basic moral intuitions about justice and punishment. When society's laws adequately punish wrongdoers, then our motive for vengeance is quenched, but when a legal system fails to properly punish wrongdoers, vengeance motivates us to achieve justice by other means. In other words, when legal justice fails, according to French, we're morally justified in seeking appropriate means of vengeful punishment.

French's argument is nuanced and complex, and he doesn't promote vengeance *carte blanche*. Instead, vengeance is seen as the careful consideration of carrying out the appropriate punishment for the wrong committed. In other words, we must treat like cases alike.

So, if Ms. Gillyflower wrongs me by murdering my wife, and the legal system fails to prosecute her—and, of course, the Doctor and Paternoster Gang aren't there to help—I have the *moral* right to exact my revenge, even if it means I wind up in jail for violating legal codes. This is where things get difficult.

She murdered my wife, so the punishment should be something similar. Yet, there appears to be no corollary punishment. First, Ms. Gillyflower didn't murder me, so me killing her isn't the same. In fact, since I have to suffer the pain of having my loved one unjustly taken away from me, killing Ms. Gillyflower might be letting her off too easy. Ms. Gillyflower robbed me of the person I love, so the like thing to do would be to murder someone she loves. The problem with this punishment is: if I murder an innocent person, then I become a murderer, and deserve to be punished for murdering an innocent person. We might say, from my wife's perspective, Ms. Gillyflower murdered her, so my killing of Ms. Gillyflower is simply me claiming the rights of my deceased wife. In such a case, I would serve as a representative of my wife, taking care of the business she was unable to complete due to Ms. Gillyflower's actions. The problem with this approach is my wife was innocent and didn't deserve death, but Ms. Gillyflower isn't innocent. Unlike my wife, she's guilty and deserves punishment. So, the killing of Ms. Gillyflower doesn't carry with it the same moral weight. Is this close enough for justice? I don't know, but I hope you're starting to see how difficult it is to "properly" punish someone, and not just randomly pick a punishment.

Once we allow for moral vengeance, we open ourselves to these sorts of difficult issues, which usually lead to blood-feuds. Legal codes serve as the foundation of civil society and are designed to avoid such issues and feuds. From the law of the Israelites found in the Hebrew scriptures to the Roman legal codes, which inspired the Germanic legal codes and eventually all of Europe and America, legal codes provide a means of escape from the cycle of violence that often erupts as a result of individuals seeking their own moral justice through vengeance.

One way to approach resolving some of these issues is to figure out the purpose of retributive justice. Is justice achieved when the proper punishment is carried out, or is it achieved when the wrongdoer is rehabilitated, or is it when wrongdoers and victims achieve reconciliation?

Which Way To The Just

A person's sense of retributive justice often depends on the "direction" in which they think justice occurs. For many, justice is backward-looking. There are a set of rules, and when one is violated, we "look back" to see exactly what happened, and dole out the appropriate punishment prescribed for such an offense. Opposed to a backward-looking approach is a forward-looking approach, which looks at the violation and determines the type of punishment that will produce the best outcome. The implications of these two approaches is vast. If you're backward-looking, then all you're interested in is the act and the prescribed punishment. Any consideration of outcomes is outside of the scope of justice. If you're forward-looking, then punishment is at best an attempt to make amends and possibly rehabilitate the perpetrator.

There are shortcomings to each approach, and instead of picking one or the other, the Doctor suggests we should develop a way of thinking about retributive justice that involves looking backwards, forwards, and "in between." In fact, the Doctor's approach shifts focus away from retributive justice (punishment), and suggests that we should primarily care about providing for people's needs, which was discussed in Chapter 2 as *distributive* justice. The Doctor's "in between" is based on his ethic of needs, which requires us to always take into account what each party needs, both wrongdoers and victims, and determine what will bring about better people and a better world. The Doctor's approach helps us avoid the implications of Isaac Asimov's mantra in *Foundation*: "Never let your sense of morals get in the way of doing what is right," for when we get so caught up in our desire for our own particular ideas of "proper" punishment, we tend to perform all sorts of unjust deeds. If we instead focus on what people need, and we train ourselves to act justly, then what we consider punishment will be transformed into something much different than we're used to in contemporary society.

Think about what might go wrong if you only take a backward-looking approach. You lose the ability to take into account any extenuating circumstances, which might tell you that the wrongdoer deserves less (or more) than the prescribed punishment. For instance, the Doctor's first on-screen action involves him abducting two school teachers ("An Unearthly Child," 1963). If you're only interested in what laws were broken, then you should respond like a good Judoon: hunt him down, and swiftly execute the proper punishment. Such an approach might work in some instances, but as in the Doctor's case, it's too harsh. It ignores all sorts of important moral features. Proper punishment requires a consideration of all the facts, motives, and extenuating circumstances, which is why a backward-looking approach by itself won't do, and why the Doctor criticizes the Judoon's type of justice.

Similar problems arise if we only take a forward-looking approach. The moral theory of utilitarianism, which tells us to maximize pleasure and minimize pain for all involved, serves as a good example of a forward-looking approach. One of the most prominent arguments against utilitarianism is that it allows for injustice. As John Rawls discusses in "Two Concepts of Rules," future consequences are the only morally relevant features a utilitarian should consider when determining punishment. Because of this, utilitarians don't care about the past. They only care about what'll bring about the most good over bad, all things considered. The downside of this moral position is that it provides a conceptual basis for punishing *innocent* people, if doing so brings about enough overall good. Such injustices will be rare, since punishing innocent people will typically bring about more pain than pleasure, especially for the innocent person who is punished. Still, this is a deeply troubling conceptual flaw.

When the Doctor abducts Ian and Barbara, what does he deserve? We might say that putting up with Ian and Barbara's hard-headedness is punishment enough, but their stubbornness was probably justified. In terms of a backward-looking approach, we would punish the Doctor for abducting Ian and Barbara, and we might punish them for forced entry into the TARDIS. In terms of a forward-looking approach, we would have to determine what punishment would bring about the most good. It's tempting just to say, the Doctor does so much good, we should let him go free, but you could also argue that a lot of the good he does is only needed because of his interfering. For instance, it's the Doctor who stirs up the Dalek "hornet's nest" in both "The Daleks" (1963) and "Genesis of the Daleks" (1975). In the Doctor's case, then, a forward-looking approach provides little guidance.

Now, if we add a needs-based analysis of the situation, we can take into account the above, and we can also look at how Ian and Barbara's travels with the Doctor enriched their lives. We can list all of the people they saved on their journeys. We can also consider how their travels influenced the Doctor to become kinder and gentler—the most popular example being when Ian prevents the Doctor from murdering the caveman in "An Unearthly Child." By focusing on needs, we're allowed to examine all of the relevant features of the case (backwards, forwards, in between) and determine that not only were Ian and Barbara not wronged by being abducted, but all things considered, everyone is better-off as a result of their nosiness and the Doctor's paranoia. Like good flâneurs, Ian, Barbara, and the Doctor were all living engaged lives, following their instincts to help a young girl. They were all trying to provide for the needs of others. As a result, they ended up joining forces, traveling together, helping others, and saving planets. They all got what they needed. We only arrive at this conclusion if we're willing to look at the case not only from a punishment point of view, but also from a needs-based point of view. By carefully examining the case, we discover no wrong has occurred; so no punishment is deserved.

Let's make things a little more difficult. What sort of punishment does the Doctor deserve from the Time Lords for stealing an old Type-40 TARDIS, violating the Time Lord policy of non-interference, and breaking the rules of time? These are serious crimes, akin to treason, and the Time Lords continually struggle with what the Doctor deserves. He's broken the law, yet he does so many good things, sometimes at the request of the Time Lords. In "The War Games" (1969), they exile him and force a regeneration. During the Tom Baker years (1974-1981) he's continually badgered to work for them, and even courted as Time Lord president—punishment indeed! In "The Trial of a Time Lord" (1986), he's put on trial for his meddling, and by the New Series he's portrayed as a nuisance—a gadfly, best ignored ("The Day of the Doctor," 2013).

Even though the Doctor has violated Time Lord law, because the Doctor is dedicated to doing good, and he actually achieves the good, the idea of punishment doesn't apply. To say the Doctor deserves punishment for doing what is just, is a misuse of language, and it's why the Time Lords struggle with how to punish him. Their backward-looking rules say one thing, their forward-looking intuitions tell them another, and in between you have the Doctor doing what's necessary to help others and to protect the universe from evil. Interestingly enough, the last act of the Time Lords (that we've seen to date) is to recognize the Doctor's good work, and grant him a new set of regenerations—justice indeed.

What have we decided, so far? First, we need to be clear about how we understand the purpose of punishment. Second, we've seen that *Doctor Who* suggests we approach justice by focusing on doing good and providing for other's needs, and when issues of retributive justice arise, we use the same approach to determine what sort of wrong has been committed and what's actually deserved.

Regular viewers of *Doctor Who* know this is only half of the story, for the Doctor also challenges us to have mercy and to forgive, both of which give wrongdoers less than they deserve. If this is true, then are mercy and forgiveness unjust?

Justice Without Punishment?

As already noted, retributive justice requires a punishment that matches the wrong committed. Yet, the Doctor's needs-based ethic often tells us to give wrongdoers less than they deserve by having compassion, showing mercy, and granting forgiveness. So, can we have justice without proper punishment? The Doctor would say, "Yes." Let's see why, and I'll let you decide if he's right.

In terms of morality, the most common punishment for victims is that of holding resentment (moral anger) towards the wrongdoer. Punishment is supposed to quench our resentment. Of course, there might be times when someone wrongs us and we don't feel resentment. A child might call the Ninth Doctor "big ears," and because it's a child, the Doctor might just ignore her; but he might resent an adult, like Mikey Smith, who did the same—he might even respond by calling him Rickey! Instead of feeling resentment and seeking punishment, we might respond by doing something like granting forgiveness and reducing the wrongdoer's punishment. Yet, if wrongdoers deserve resentment, and forgiveness forswears resentment, then forgiveness is unjust, because the wrongdoer doesn't get what he deserves.

The Doctor's needs-based ethic asks us to look *back* at the wrong committed, then look *forward* to what will bring about the best consequences. In between these two considerations, we must also examine the needs of the wrongdoer, in order to determine the character and needs of the person. The Doctor's approach recognizes that a wrong has been committed and deserves a punishment. It then examines the needs of the wrongdoer (and victim) to determine what other moral features must be taken into consideration. Finally, it takes all of the information and arrives at a punishment that takes into account all morally relevant information and suggests a punishment that's not only best for, but also what's needed by, all parties involved.

Think of Commander Lytton, who appeared in two episodes: "Resurrection of the Daleks" (1984) and "Attack of the Cybermen" (1985). In the former episode, he aided the Daleks in their rescue of Davros. In the latter episode, he appears to aid the Cybermen in their plot to crash Halley's Comet into Earth, thereby, preventing the destruction of Mondas in "The Tenth Planet" (1966). Throughout both stories, Lytton is portrayed as the evil collaborator, only concerned with his own gain. He fights with the Doctor, and the Doctor does his best to thwart his plans. However, by the end of "Attack of the Cybermen" we find out that Lytton is helping the Cryons fight against the Cybermen. After discovering his mistake, the Doctor realizes he's "never misjudged anyone quite so badly..."

Lytton provides a nice example of how we don't always know the motives behind people's actions. In fact, with Lytton it's unclear how much of Lytton still exists after the Dalek "conditioning" that occurs in "Resurrection of the Daleks." What's clear is that the Doctor is anguished over his resentment and desire to punish Lytton. Even though Lytton committed several immoral acts, the Doctor's awareness of the *entire* situation suggests that if Lytton had survived, the Doctor would've forgiven his actions and let him go without any sort of punishment. He does the same for Sabalom Glitz ("The Trial of a Time Lord" and "Dragonfire," 1987), and arguably, Rusty in "Into the Dalek" (2014). The Doctor sees something within these immoral agents, and instead of giving them the punishment they deserve, he does something different. He tries to reform and help them reach their full potential. As we see with Rusty, it doesn't always work, but that's part of the process. The Doctor's ethic of need doesn't require us to be successful, but it does challenge us to try.

The key then is to show how the Doctor's account of distributive justice—his ethic of need—is consistent with retributive justice; that giving wrongdoers less than they deserve is just. In the book *Justice in Love*, Nicholas Wolterstorff provides a useful distinction between pure retributive punishment and what he refers to as "reprobative punishment." Where retribution is considered backward-looking, reprobative punishment attempts to do what we see the Doctor do: "to condemn what was done and to send a message of non-condonation." Reprobative punishment, then, is a type of punishment that is concerned with the welfare of the wrongdoer—it accepts the repentance of the wrongdoer, and seeks a lesser punishment designed to respect both the wrongdoer and the victim. So, when someone commits a wrongful act, the Doctor doesn't just condemn them to such-and-such punishment. Instead, he investigates their motives and knowledge, while trying to understand and reform them, in order for them to receive what they deserve and (if possible) flourish.

Think of all of the examples covered in the previous chapter on evil. In each case, he investigates, learns, and offers them a way out. From "vampires" in Venice ("Vampires in Venice," 2010) and gaseous aliens in Cardiff ("The Unquiet Dead," 2005), to two-dimensional creatures in Bristol ("Flatline"), the Doctor offers help, and in order to help, he must know what these aliens need. He doesn't condone the wrongful actions of invaders, but as we see in "Flatline," he recognizes they may not understand the extent to which they are wronging other moral beings. So, he sets his energies towards finding a way of stopping the invaders, one that respects their moral worth. Even when he finds invaders to be evil, he most-often offers them an escape. Of course, when they fail to take the escape, the Doctor stops them because he's the Doctor and he's "the man that stops the monsters."

Reprobative justice is a type of retributive justice that incorporates the consideration of the needs of the wrongdoer and victim, and looks for ways that allow both to flourish. Such an approach is difficult, and it doesn't always produce the exact results that you expect. Just like every other aspect of our life, we're vulnerable to having injustice result from our attempts to be just. We can either not try, or we can develop a habit of learning from our mistakes and committing to making better decisions in the future. The Doctor would never tell us to give up, so when faced with trying to bring about justice, we must work towards doing the best we can. This might imply that our journey's over, but it isn't. We have one more path to journey down, and it's the path of forgiveness, especially of self-forgiveness.

The Doctor's Journey To Forgiveness

Forgiveness is one of humanity's most complex moral concepts. On one hand, it's deeply personal. Each one of us has an idea of what forgiveness is and when and how we should forgive. On the other hand, forgiveness is fundamentally relational. It involves other people, even if the "other person" is yourself. So, no matter how personal forgiveness is, it's always a relational concept. As seen in the previous section, forgiveness is sometimes at odds with justice, since forgiveness tells us to give wrongdoers less than they deserve. Reprobative justice helps to some degree, by illustrating that wrongdoers sometimes deserve mercy and forgiveness. Forgiveness, however, can at times be so extreme that it offers no punishment at all, or a punishment so different that it doesn't seem to fit the deed. Let's look at some of the issues, especially those relating to the Doctor's inner-turmoil and attempt to forgive himself.

For the most part, Classic *Doctor Who* doesn't have a lot to say about forgiveness, but by the time you get to the New Series, forgiveness and its related concepts take center stage. The Doctor now apologizes to enemies, seeks the redemption of friends and enemies alike, and maybe most importantly, longs to be rid of the torment and guilt of his actions during the last Great Time War. He wants the peace and reconciliation that forgiveness promises. The Time War, along with the 50th Anniversary Special "The Day of the Doctor," allow us to frame the Doctor's life as one long journey. Resembling the Christian parable of the prodigal son, his journey hasn't been easy, nor does he always make the right decisions; but in the end, he comes to terms with who he is, is accepted by his people, and he's even granted a new set of regenerations. Of course, we must wait to see how all of this plays out, but for now, the Doctor seems to have found himself cleared of past transgressions.

Nevertheless, the Doctor's journey hasn't been easy, and I'd like to examine two particular episodes, which I take to be parables of the Doctor's self-punishment and his journey towards self-forgiveness. The first episode is "Dinosaurs on a Spaceship" (2012). In this episode, the Doctor encounters Solomon, a space "trader"—in other words, pirate—who not only hijacked a Silurian spaceship but also ejected them into space. Solomon didn't kill the Silurians because of some deeply held ideological belief or because he thought they were evil. No, he killed them because they stood in the way of something he wanted: profit. Solomon knew what he was doing, and he knew it was wrong. Yet, he did it anyway, and even delighted in doing it. If that wasn't enough, he shoots the triceratops right in front of the Doctor with the same cool, disinterested greed. So, when it came time for Solomon to be punished, the Doctor showed no hesitation punishing him to death.

It isn't shocking to see Solomon executed—your intuitions probably tell you he deserves it. What's shocking is that the Eleventh Doctor condemns Solomon to death so easily. Something has changed, which is exactly what Amy Pond points out in the next episode "A Town Called Mercy" (2012):

> **The Doctor**: We could end this right now. We could save everyone right now!
> **Amy**: This is not how we roll, and you know it. What's happened to you, Doctor? When did killing someone become an option?
> **The Doctor**: Jex has to answer for his crimes.
> **Amy**: And what then? Are you going to hunt down everyone who's made a gun or a bullet or a bomb?
> **The Doctor**: But they keep coming back, don't you see? Every time I negotiate, I try to understand. Well not today. No, today I honor the victims first. His, the Master's, the Daleks'. All the people that died because of my mercy!
> **Amy**: See this is what happens when you travel alone for too long. Well listen to me, Doctor, we can't be like him. We have to be better than him.

Notice how pained the Doctor is by his "mercy." He's seen the result of his mercy, and he's tired of seeing it lead to the deaths of innocent people. This is such a powerful moment because it illustrates not only the Doctor's vulnerability, but also the difficulties of reprobative punishment. During his time of weakness, he's come to the conclusion that it's easier just to kill off villains, and he's right: it is easier. There's no questioning or thinking. It's kill quickly and move on, just like we saw in "Dinosaurs on a Spaceship." Amy points out the flaw in his logic: once you say, "Execute those who cause killing," then we must start executing all killers. We start with the killers, move to the makers of weapons, and end with the people who pay taxes, which support the manufacturers and governments involved in killing. This line of reasoning might be good for some, but it isn't for the Doctor. It's not how he rolls.

In "A Town Called Mercy," Kahler-Jex serves as a mirror of the Doctor. Jex killed many innocent people in order to create a weapon that would bring about peace, by killing millions of enemies. When Jex stands up to the Doctor, defiantly defending his war crimes, the Doctor hears his own attempt to justify the killing of millions to achieve peace, and he sees its hollowness. Just as the Doctor would like to eradicate "the Doctor" who committed those crimes, he sets out to eradicate *doctor* Jex.

One clever conceptual twist in the episode is that Kahler-Tek, the Gunslinger, also mirrors the Doctor. Tek wants revenge on the person who ruined his life and caused him to kill millions, and he's willing to "tear the universe apart" in order to achieve his own peace. These two characters illustrate the struggle that goes on within the Doctor's psyche. As made clear in "The Day of the Doctor," the Doctor is at war with himself. He's yet to be punished for his deeds during the Time War, and his internal battle manifests itself in "A Town Called Mercy."

Forgiveness doesn't occur in "A Town Called Mercy," but the first step towards forgiveness happens, and it's mercy. Jex breaks the cycle of violence and hatred by recognizing Tek, and by ending his own life, in order to save Tek from having one more death on his conscience. Freed from the torment of his revenge, Tek is able to not only find his own personal peace, but he also becomes an agent of peace, protecting the people of Mercy. This is what the Doctor needs.

After the execution of Solomon, the Doctor too is able to take the first step towards forgiveness. With Amy's reminder and Jex's and Tek's examples, the Doctor finds himself one step closer to coming to terms with his actions during the Time War. It's with all of this inner-turmoil in mind that the Eleventh Doctor's refusal to use the Moment in "The Day of the Doctor" becomes his moment of peace. It's the peace of resolving his inner-turmoil that gives him the opportunity to recognize himself in the War Doctor. He's able to wipe the slate clean by "killing" the War Doctor, through the act of recognizing him as the man who was the Doctor on the day it was impossible to be the Doctor. It's this step towards self-forgiveness that reinvigorates his life of protecting the universe. So, if we understand the Doctor's fictional tale of avoiding the mass extermination of the Time Lords as a parable for how we must find ways to work through our own inner-turmoil, maybe one day we too can forgive, stop punishing ourselves, and begin to flourish.

I'm Going Home

I wish to end with a story of punishment from Arun Gandhi (Mahatma Gandhi's grandson). In a short piece entitled "A Recollection," Arun reminisces about taking his father to an all-day conference. While at the conference, he was supposed to get the car serviced. As many kids would do, he played around, saw a movie, and showed up several hours late to retrieve his father. Expecting to get in trouble, he lied to his father about why he was late, saying the garage took longer to repair the car than he expected. His father recognized the lie, and instead of punishing Arun, punished himself; saying, "There's something wrong in the way I brought you up that didn't give you the confidence to tell me the truth. In order to figure out where I went wrong with you, I'm going to walk home 18 miles and think about it." His father's self-punishment changed Arun's life forever, inspiring him to travel the globe teaching lessons on peace and non-violence. It's this sort of thoughtful engagement with the people who morally wrong us that the Doctor is trying to teach.

Some events in our lives forever change us, whether those events are caused by people around us or caused by ourselves. We must learn how to respond to being wronged. We must realize that traveling the moral landscape isn't always easy, nor is it always pleasant. We must look for companions that will travel with us on our journeys. But once we begin engaging life properly, and begin working through our own personal moral challenges, we'll find new ways of looking at punishment, justice, revenge, and yes, even forgiveness and self-forgiveness.

References:

Episodes:
Doctor Who:
> "An Unearthly Child" (1963)
> "The Daleks" (1963)
> "The Tenth Planet" (1966)
> "The War Games" (1969)
> "Genesis of the Daleks" (1975)
> "Resurrection of the Daleks" (1984)
> "Attack of the Cybermen" (1985)
> "The Trial of a Time Lord" (1986)
> "Dragonfire" (1987)
> "The Unquiet Dead" (2005)
> "The Vampires of Venice" (2010)
> "Dinosaurs on a Spaceship" (2012)
> "A Town Called Mercy" (2012)
> "The Crimson Horror" (2013)
> "The Day of the Doctor" (2013)
> "Into the Dalek" (2014)
> "Flatline" (2014)

Authors:
Asimov, Isaac. (1966). *Foundation*. New York: Avon Books; Originally published in 1951.

French, Peter A. (1997). *Cowboy Metaphysics: Ethics and Death in Westerns*. Lanham, MD: Rowman & Littlefield Publishers.

_____. (2001). *The Virtues of Vengeance*. Kansas: University Press of Kansas.

Gandhi, Arun. (Accessed July 2015). "A Recollection." http://www.google.com/url?sa=t&rct=j&q=&esrc=s&source=web&cd=1&ved=0CB8QFjAA&url=http%3A%2F%2Fwww.panoreon.gr%2Ffiles%2Fitems%2F3%2F365%2Fa_recollection_dr_arun_gandhi.pdf&ei=ZhygVfjrDsmS-wHJ-YCQBQ&usg=AFQjCNFnC27Ifqk1m92BnRjDxAbzVYdHCw&sig2=2w

MCDnyeBvZksJhE-Cje_A&bvm=bv.96952980,d.cWw

Rawls, John. (1955). "Two Concepts of Rules." *The Philosophical Review*. Volume 64.

Wolterstorff, Nicholas. (2011). *Justice in Love* (Emory University Studies in Law and Religion). Grand Rapids: William B. Eerdmans Publishing.

6

KNOW THY DOCTOR

> There is something about the type of imagination that powers *Doctor Who* that sweeps up viewers and inspires them in unexpected ways. Something about its mix of the fantastic and the mundane, the far-flung with the domestic, that is unlike anything else.
>
> —David Tennant

One of the most interesting fields of study in philosophy, especially because of its clever and abstract thought experiments, is epistemology. 'Epistemology' comes from the Greek *episteme*, meaning 'knowledge', and is the study of knowledge and justified belief. Though questions concerning what counts as knowledge were asked by the earliest philosophers, theories of justified belief and knowledge began to flourish in the past century, especially with the argumentative proof that a justified true belief fails to count as knowledge. We might even say that epistemology and *Doctor Who* flourished together over the past five or six decades.

Due to the abstract nature of epistemology, and the fact that the Doctor rarely stops to explain why and how he knows something, this chapter will be presented in a slightly different manner than the other chapters. Instead of crafting a careful argument for why the Doctor accepts or rejects certain epistemic theories, I will simply provide an overview of the subject and offer some general suggestions for how the Doctor might respond. In other words, I will play the role of the companion and epistemology will be the Doctor, which means the concepts and issues of epistemology will take center stage while I try to help the audience understand what's being said and done. For the most part, I will refrain from drawing any specific conclusions about the Doctor's epistemic position, but near the end I will offer a suggestion that the imagination plays an important role in what counts as knowledge. As we begin, it's alright to be scared, just don't be scared away. You must have courage, for as the Third Doctor tell us, "Courage isn't just a matter of not being frightened... It's being afraid and doing what you have to do anyway" ("Planet of the Daleks," 1973).

Learning the Lingo

In the early 90's I used to dress up as the Doctor for Halloween, and no one knew who I was supposed to be. Since I typically wore a scarf, or an old checkered jacket, they'd often say, "Did you just fly in from the alps?" I would just shake my head, and say, "No, I'm a different kind of doctor—the Doctor!" They still didn't understand.

To avoid such confusion, let's spend some time making sure we understand the language of epistemology. First, there are many senses of the term 'know'. I might know you from a convention, or I can know how to play guitar, or I can know that the Doctor is from Gallifrey. The last type of knowledge is called "propositional knowledge," and is the most prominent type of knowledge examined by epistemologists. Since the object of propositional knowledge is a proposition (meaning it's either true or false), epistemologists can clearly examine what is said, in order to determine if it is, or if it can be knowable.

To better understand knowledge, we must separate it from belief. First, as Kevin McCain notes in *The Nature of Scientific Knowledge*, knowledge requires belief. You can't know the Doctor is a Time Lord, if you don't have a belief that the Doctor's a Time Lord. However, belief doesn't imply knowledge. I can believe that

Cybermen are on their way to invade Earth, but without some sort of further evidence, I can't say I know it. My belief that Cyberman are coming, whether a desire or fear, is mere opinion. Not all belief is mere opinion, for belief can be grounded in factual occurrences that provide support for my belief. For instance, I can believe *Doctor Who* will be renewed next season, and though I can't know it with any certainty until it is actually renewed, due to its track record of being renewed, my belief is stronger than mere opinion. It's similar to a physician who uses their knowledge of medicine and healing to form a belief about your sickness. We might incorrectly refer to it as a "medical opinion," but a physician's diagnosis of my physical state is much stronger than my unfounded desire/fear that the Cybermen are coming.

Second, "knowledge' implies truth, while 'belief' does not. When I say "I know the Doctor exists," I'm making a claim that implies I both have a belief about the Doctor and that it is true. Before discussing how something gains the status of truth, let's look a little closer at my claim to believe the Doctor exists. There are two ways in which you might believe something. I can believe *that* the Doctor exists, which means I have a certain mental state or opinion that there's an actual time-traveling alien who busies himself saving the universe, or I can believe *in* the Doctor, which means I believe in what the Doctor stands for and represents. Again, as pointed out by McCain, knowledge requires "belief that," not "belief in." I can believe (or have "faith in," as McCain says) in many things relating to the Doctor's character without actually believing that a Time Traveling alien actually exists. Whether I believe that or in something will affect the nature of the knowledge I claim to have about a thing.

There's a part of me that hopes the belief that the Doctor exists is true, but I actually believe in the Doctor. Such a belief is what David Holley calls "life-orienting," because it shapes my life, and as a result, it's easy for me to *know* my belief in the Doctor is true. My life is influenced by how I watch and interpret the show, and because this belief is central to who I am, I often make knowledge claims regarding *Doctor Who*. The book you're currently holding in your hands is full of them. Regardless of my belief about the Doctor, when I make a knowledge claim I'm asserting that I have good evidence for why it is true. I'm saying more than just "It's my opinion," I'm suggesting I can offer good reasons as "proof" for my belief. Epistemology refers to this "proof" as justification and/or warrant.

The Proof of Justification

Imagine you're the Doctor's companion, and he runs off to get something from his TARDIS. Of course, being a companion, you strike up a conversation with some seedy looking bald guy in a toga, who calls himself Socrates. While talking, he asks, "What is knowledge?" After thinking, you respond, "It's whatever I see." This might at first seem like a good answer, but there are three reasons why it isn't. First, knowledge can't be mere seeing, since such an answer implies when we close our eyes we become ignorant. Second, and more importantly, there are many things we can't see (unless we write them out!), yet we know—e.g., $2 + 2 = 4$. Finally, our sight might be mistaken. Imagine you look off in the distance, see someone who resembles the Doctor, and say, "See, there's the Doctor returning from his TARDIS." However, when the figure gets closer it becomes clear that it was someone else with impeccable style heading your direction. These three reasons show that knowledge must be something else.

Since seeing and perceiving play such fundamental roles in the way we know the world, adding something to them might provide a justification for knowledge. One thing that we might add is a judgment about what we perceive. If you put your thumb in front of your eye, it will look much bigger than most of your surroundings: It will cover other people's heads, the sun, and even a Dalek off in the distance. Your perception suggests your thumb is bigger, but your judgment (i.e. reason) tells you it's an illusion. Such judgment might save your life in the occurrence of a real Dalek heading your way—run! Judgment (often seen as a kind of belief), then, plays some role in knowledge, especially if the judgement is true. Instead of haphazardly claiming "the Doctor is approaching," because the person resembles the Doctor and you know he's on his way back from the TARDIS, careful critical thinkers will withhold judgment until he's closer, so they can be certain they KNOW he's coming. In this way, judgment helps ensure knowledge.

The main question now is, does knowledge require certainty? If you say you know the answer to $2 + 2$, then you know it with certainty that it's 4. You know it so well, you could even demonstrate it to others. According to Socrates, in Plato's dialogue *Meno*, your ability to demonstrate proves you know what you say you know; that's why teachers give so many tests.

Demonstration and proof, however, come in many different forms. If you want to prove that "all unmarried Doctors are bachelors," you need only ponder the concept of Doctor (married or unmarried male) and bachelor (unmarried male) to determine whether it's true. By definition, it is true, since unmarried men are bachelors—married men can't be bachelors. On the other hand, if you want to prove that your thumb is smaller than a Dalek, you will have walk up to the Dalek and compare the two—though it might be the last thing you do. Within this explanation, however, lies the problem. Even with the best of judgments, we can still be wrong. Deductive truths, like mathematics, geometry and logic can be known and demonstrated with certainty, but inductive truths, like comparing your thumb's size to a Dalek, lack any such certainty.

This brings us to the important distinction between the knowledge generated through deductive and inductive reasoning. Deductive reasoning provides for certainty, assuming one's reasoning is sound. It's used in mathematics, geometry, logic, and the conceptual analysis of ideas, like unmarried men and bachelors. Inductive reasoning, however, is based on experience, like judging the proper size of your thumb compared to a Dalek. Inductive reasoning doesn't provide certainty, but if used properly can provide strong evidence for the probability of a conclusion. For instance, based on your prior experience of seeing Daleks, which gives you a strong indication of how large they are compared to your thumb, you can use your judgment to conclude that your thumb is smaller than a Dalek. Such a belief can't be known with certainty, for it's possible for Daleks to be tiny, but experience tells us such a possibility is highly improbable.

Inductive vs. deductive reasoning creates some intriguing conundrums for epistemologists, especially concerning the possibility of certain knowledge based on our human inductive experience of the world. Let's see how Edmund Gettier revolutionized epistemology, just as *Doctor Who* revolutionized television.

The Trouble With A Logical TARDIS

Knowledge as justified true belief remained the norm for epistemologists until Gettier's 1963 essay, "Is Justified True Belief Knowledge?" Gettier's first argument goes something like this: Imagine the Doctor is going to pick his new companion today, and it's come down to you and Bill. From your snooping, you develop excellent reasons for thinking that Bill will be the next companion— you heard the Doctor say that it will be Bill, Bill told you that she would be the next companion, and so on. Since you know that Bill has a blue jean jacket, and you have excellent reason to think that she will be the next companion, you correctly reason that the next companion will have a blue jean jacket. In other words, you have a justified true belief that the next companion will have a blue jean jacket.

Here comes the fun part. Imagine further that you, in fact, own a blue jean jacket, and the Doctor plans on picking you instead of Bill. It turns out that you are wrong about Bill being the next companion, you are the next companion! But, as it happens your belief that the next companion has a blue jean jacket is true because you have a blue jean jacket. So, your belief that the next companion has a blue jean jacket is both justified (you have good reason to believe it) and true, but it isn't knowledge. You didn't "know" that the next companion will have a blue jean jacket, even though it's a justified true belief. As a result, we've shown that justified true beliefs don't guarantee certain knowledge. A sad state of affairs, indeed, if you wish knowledge to be certain!

Instead of jettisoning knowledge altogether, it's wiser to reject the requirement that knowledge be certain. In fact, since Gettier, many epistemologists have offered accounts of justification designed to show we can have knowledge without certainty, focusing instead on what conditions must be met for knowledge to be warranted. Let's take a brief journey through the history of philosophy to examine some prominent areas of epistemology.

Rebuilding The Universe's Knowledge

René Descartes (1596-1650) famously argued, "I think, therefore, I am." With this argument, Descartes shows that we, as thinking things, exist beyond any sort of doubt. Even if everything in existence is doubted (the senses, the physical world, and even mathematics), there must be something doing the doubting (i.e. thinking). This doubting occurs as an idea in my mind, and to have ideas means there must be some thinking thing having those ideas. I, therefore, know that, as a thinking thing, I must exist.

Descartes's argument still influences contemporary society, and can be seen in several *Doctor Who* episodes, such as "The Last Christmas" (2014), where the characters know they exist, but can't decide which external existence is real. Descartes is important for our purposes for two reasons. First, he made certainty the goal of knowledge, and second, he is a Classical Foundationalist. As a Classical Foundationalist, he maintains that knowledge is justified by having a belief (or set of beliefs) not justified by other beliefs. "I think, therefore, I am" (often called the Cogito, since the Latin is "cogito, ergo, sum") is one such belief. The Cogito requires no further beliefs to be true, so it serves as a foundation for the rest of knowledge. To deny the Cogito, serves only to justify it further; for to have a belief requires a thinking thing to have a belief about denying a belief. Descartes's foundationalism has been challenged by many over the centuries. Let's look at two.

David Hume (1711-1776) distinguished between inductive and deductive reasoning, and argued that knowledge based on experience can only be known by induction. Many of the beliefs we know to be true—the sun will rise in the east, my car will start, *Doctor Who* will be renewed for another season—can't be known with certainty. Nature can always change, cars break, and TV executives make stupid decisions. However, if we're careful with the claims and assumptions we make, beliefs can be true with a high degree of probability. So, until *Doctor Who* shows signs of being canceled, my belief in its renewal is strong.

Hume agreed that we can know deductive truths, like math, logic, and geometry, with certainty, but his work showed that most of human knowledge is markedly different. We'll see below that Hume's arguments suggest a new approach to knowledge, one based on the rational coherence of beliefs.

Finally, Thomas Reid (1710-1796) suggested we dispense with the Cartesian "way of ideas" that separates the mind from the world implied by the Cogito, and instead, focus on the direct perception of the external world. According to Reid, Descartes's insistence on the existence of a thinking thing (a self/consciousness) that only perceives the world via its perception of ideas in the mind leads to a skepticism of the external world's existence. Reid's arguments for how it is possible to perceive the world directly will suggest an approach to epistemology that allows for knowledge to result from our natural perception and engagement with the world. This approach, then, allows for beliefs justified by reliable belief-generating devices, like the senses, and this concept is known as reliabilism.

Justification Regenerated

Our main question remains, what justifies belief, thereby, making it knowledge? Based directly or indirectly on the work of the philosophers just examined (and many others), the past forty years offer some intriguing answers.

Beginning with the work of William Alston in the 1970s, foundationalism underwent a regeneration of its own. Addressing the criticism of arbitrary beliefs, in "Two Types of Foundationalism," Alston argues for a foundationalism, similar to Reid's work, based on our perception and engagement with the world. For Alston, we have a certain level of knowledge that occurs simply as a result of our biological connection to our surroundings. As a result, there are two "levels" of knowledge: a) a lower level that occurs immediately through perception; and b) a higher level that occurs when we reflect upon our ideas and/or try to justify why we know something to be true. To illustrate, imagine you see the TARDIS as you walk through the park. How do you know that you see the TARDIS? Well, you know it because you're actually perceiving it. Assuming you're not sick, hallucinating, or on a film set, your perceptual abilities reliably give you information about the world, and in this instance they tell you that you're seeing the TARDIS. Do you know this with certainty? No. But if you senses are reliable, then Alston maintains that you have an immediate belief that counts as knowledge, at least on a lower level.

Not all knowledge occurs on this lower level. Humans have the ability to reflect on their beliefs, and if needed, provide justifications. The ability and need to justify beliefs illustrates how humans also have a higher level of knowledge. Seeing the TARDIS is a pretty shocking event, so much so that if it were to occur, your mind would probably shift instantly into a higher level or reasoning. You would investigate to see if it were the genuine article or a knock off. The same thing would happen, if someone asked "how do you know you saw the TARDIS?" Any time you reflect on a belief or provide justifications for a belief, you're using higher level epistemic reasoning.

Alston's discussion of levels of knowledge illustrates the difference between *being* justified and *showing* that one is justified. In cases where you properly perceive something, you are justified by the process of perception. When you reflect, or your belief is challenged, you are justified by the process of proving (i.e. showing) your belief to yourself or others.

In a general way, allowing for a lower level of knowledge supports the conception of reality shown in *Doctor Who*. If only those capable of higher level reasoning can be said to have knowledge, then we must doubt the possibility of children, animals, adults with cognitive disabilities, and a whole host of aliens having knowledge. Any being incapable of providing justifications for their beliefs must be said to lack knowledge, and this inability would influence their moral status, because it implies an inferiority to those who are capable of higher level reasoning. The Doctor is continually giving creatures the benefit of doubt, respecting their ability to understand and know what is best for them. Even when he encounters a group who is unwilling to listen to his pleas, he uses methods to help them understand.

Alston's foundationalism addresses the criticism of Classical Foundationalism that foundational beliefs are arbitrary by grounding beliefs in the non-arbitrary belief-generating process of our senses. Since certainty is too much to ask in terms of justification, reliabilism provides strong support for how we know certain things and why we know them.

Some worry that reliabilism is too weak to support a rich epistemology. For instance, Keith Lehrer suggests that reliabilism only allows for the incorporation of information, not knowledge, and he uses the example of Mr. Truetemp to illustrate. Without knowing, Mr. Truetemp has a device implanted in his head that allows him to get accurate temperature readings. The device allows him to have reliable information about the external temperature transferred directly from the device to his "belief center," without any further conscious consideration on his part. Mr. Truetemp "just knows" the temperature without thinking, and he's incapable of explaining how he has this information. Lehrer suggests that such an account of knowledge is flawed because Mr. Truetemp does not have knowledge, he just has information about the temperature. He "knows" the temperature, like an automated door "knows" someone is entering the building.

Mr. Truetemp kind of sounds like a character the Doctor might help on one of his adventures, and even though many take him to show reliability isn't sufficient for knowledge, reliabilists disagree. For a reliabilist, Lehrer commits a level confusion by requiring that Mr. Truetemp go beyond *being* justified by his perception to *showing* why he is justified in knowing the temperature. Mr. Truetemp's belief is justified by the process of how he comes to have the belief, not by being able to give reasons for why he has the belief. If I see a Judoon coming at me with a gun, I'm justified in my belief that he's coming at me, even if I can't explain the visual process of perception. If I could, then my belief would be that much stronger; but to know and react to the oncoming Judoon doesn't require me to have a higher level of knowledge. Mr. Truetemp's belief about the temperature is arguably sufficient for reliabilists to produce a lower level of knowledge, just as you're justified in knowing that you're hungry, or a dog is justified in knowing it's going for a walk when the leash appears.

Of course, reliabilism isn't the only option. As McCain discusses, Evidentialism offers the intuitively plausible claim that you know when your belief fits the evidence to which you have access. When you have evidence for a belief, then you're justified in believing it; and when your evidence is insufficient, you're unjustified. Unlike reliabilism, which focuses on how external objects are perceived, Evidentialism focuses on the internal states of our minds, which makes it an "Internalist" theory of justification. A reliabilist would say you know you see the TARDIS when your perception of the TARDIS is reliably formed, and you can further justify your belief (at a higher level) by examining the big blue box that you believe is the TARDIS. For an evidentialist, however, your perception of the TARDIS is evidence for your belief, because your internal mental states are of perceiving the TARDIS. Of course, there might be counter-evidence that would discount the truth of your belief: You might be sick and hallucinating, you might be on a movie set, you might have forgotten that *Doctor Who* is just a TV show—Is it? So, for Evidentialism, beliefs are justified when you have good evidence for a belief.

Another Internalist theory of justification is coherentism. Inspired by the criticism that the basic beliefs of foundationalism are arbitrary, coherence theory argues that beliefs are justified when they form a "web" of mutually supporting, internally coherent beliefs. As we'll see in the next section, some epistemologists complain that coherentism is fundamentally flawed—if each belief justifies the other, then each belief justifies itself; in other words, coherentism's justification is based on circular reasoning. McCain explains that such a criticism would only be true, if beliefs are understood in a linear fashion where an individual belief A justifies B, B justifies C, and C justifies A. This is circular reasoning and should be avoided. However, coherentism avoids circularity by maintaining beliefs are justified as a whole. Instead of focusing on the truth of individual beliefs, all beliefs should be examined as a coherent whole; and when all beliefs cohere (fit together in a reasonable way), then each individual belief is justified.

The Infiniteness of Knowledge

Before concluding the chapter, I want to make a case for a theory of justification that I think the Doctor would be inclined to accept, or at least he'd be fascinated by its cleverness. Over the past two decades, Peter Klein has argued for infinitism, which he maintains avoids the criticisms of foundationalism, knowledge resting on arbitrary beliefs, and coherence theory, the circularity of beliefs. We just saw how arbitrariness of belief can be ignored by employing reliabilism, so we can focus on circularity.

In one of Klein's more recent writings he implies the necessity of reliabilism for knowledge, but in terms of explaining the nature of human knowledge, which is a distinct feature of human knowledge, he maintains that human epistemic agents should be capable of calling on and giving reasons for why they hold certain beliefs over others. Because Klein limits the requirements of infinitism to the distinctive nature of human knowledge, which will apply to all other similar creatures, he doesn't diminish the knowledge of non-human creatures. As noted above, this is an important implication for any description of the *Doctor Who* universe. For Klein, then, in order to have a justified set of reasons, and to avoid the circularity of a belief justifying itself (I saw the TARDIS because I saw the TARDIS), our justifications must be based on an infinite number of non-repeating beliefs.

To avoid circularity, infinitism doesn't allow a person to reuse beliefs. If we can't reuse beliefs, then we must have access to an infinity of beliefs to justify our knowledge. This is a major problem, since we, as humans, are finite creatures. Due to the nature of infinity, we could spend our entire life reciting the set of all whole numbers, and we would never reach the "end," since the set of all numbers is infinite. Herein lies the cleverness of Klein's infinitism: the complaint that finite creatures can't accomplish an infinite task is based on a "completion requirement," which as Jeremy Fantl shows in "Modest Infinitism," justification not only comes in degrees, but infinitism doesn't have such a completion requirement.

Infinitism is more interested in the process than the end, which sounds a lot like our favorite Time Lord, who hates endings too. Infinitism takes into account human finiteness, and relies on the human imagination to examine beliefs for defeaters in order to arrive at knowledge. Infinitism's reliance on the imagination is one of the reasons I think the Doctor would be so intrigued by its methods.

The human brain is continually active, whether we're aware of it or not. We're constantly perceiving the world, while our brains actively process the data from our senses. Even if we're just wandering around on "autopilot," our brain is aware and constantly testing our perceptions. Just think of watching a *Doctor Who* episode, and how easy it is to relax and get lost in the story without being aware of your surroundings or the common "noises" in your head. Whether on a lower or higher level of reasoning, humans have at their disposal an infinite number of propositions that can test any belief. You could never access them all, but infinitism doesn't require that you be capable of doing so.

Let's see how this works. If you lived in Britain during the 1950s and 1960s, seeing a blue police box wouldn't be surprising. You would perceive them on a lower level without giving them a second thought, because your brain would be trained to perceive them as part of the natural surroundings. Fast forward to today, and seeing a police box, whether you're a fan of *Doctor Who* or not, instantly kicks your mind into high gear, asking: What is it? Is it a TARDIS? Is it real? Is it a fan creation? Is there a convention in town? Are they filming in town? Is this what I've been waiting for my whole life; the Doctor's come to ask me to become a companion? All of these and more illustrate how we use the imagination to ask questions about what's being perceived. The mind is looking for defeaters, some sort of explanation that will help you understand and know what you're seeing. Granted, many of the questions would be outlandish, like "Is it a car? Is it a book? Is it the number 2?", but nevertheless, they all serve to justify your belief in what you see? The mind doesn't have to actually ask every question, but thanks to the imagination, it has the capacity, if given an infinity of time, for an infinite amount of questions.

As Jacob Bronowski suggests in *The Origins of Knowledge and Imagination*, human language allows for individuals to become the subject of his or her own sentence. We are able to place ourselves in our own "box," and our imaginations give us the ability to reach out into an infinity of "open spaces." These open spaces are new ideas and beliefs generated by the imagination, which allow us access to an infinite number of positive and negative possibilities. It's this imaginative approach—placing oneself in a "box" to achieve infinity—that makes me think the Doctor would find infinitism most intriguing.

Why Is Knowledge Relevant?

Much of what I've said about the Doctor in this chapter is speculative and fairly abstract. In fact, as any good Cyber-Leader would do, I deleted several topics. There was simply no room to include a full discussion of realism (a mind-independent world exists) and anti-realism (the world is mind-dependent), the Internalist vs. Externalist debate, correspondence, pragmatic, and deflationary conceptions of truth, and a plethora of other epistemologists and epistemological theories of justification. With that in mind, let me draw to a close by offering some practical implications and lessons for how what we've discussed is involved in living the good life.

First, there's nothing wrong with being ignorant, but one should never be willfully ignorant. The more information we have, the better decisions we'll make about how to live our lives. So, the more knowledge the better. If you lack knowledge, or you don't know what counts as knowledge, you'll struggle to know anything. Hopefully, this chapter will aid in your search for truth, and to help you understand when you know something, or when you need to spend more time searching.

Second, the reliabilism of Alston's foundationalism and the imagination of Klein's infinitism suggest an engaged life of seeking and questioning. This implication is at the heart of the Doctor's other lessons, so it should be at the heart of our epistemological lesson.

Third, we can't always determine truth and knowledge by ourselves. We need the help of others. As communal beings we often arrive at an understanding of questions through what John Hardwig calls "knowledge-as-trust." Hardwig is most interested in how knowledge is generated in a scientific community through the reliable transference of data and information between multiple parties, but his conclusion applies to all human interaction. Knowledge requires we listen, test, and ultimately trust that if we're careful enough we can come to have knowledge.

Finally, there's a certain virtue to seeking knowledge. As Linda Zagzebski shows, an accurate engaged search for truth and knowledge is more than just a task, it's a sign of a person's character. Courageously seeking truth and knowledge and not shying away from difficult questions and answers is a sign of a virtuous character, while ignoring tough questions and blindly running away from truth and knowledge illustrates a poor character. The Doctor calls us to work towards the former in all that we do, regardless of whether it's in terms of ethics, art, or knowledge.

So, if you've found that you can't get enough of epistemology and all of its related conundrums, I recommend going and doing some more research. Kevin McCain's *The Nature of Scientific Knowledge*, which provides an excellent and in-depth review of the issues discussed above and many more, would make a nice companion. Other than that, it's time to move on to the Doctor's next lesson.

Notes:
A special thank you to Jared Byer, who inspired and suggested the addition

of this chapter, and Kevin McCain for his invaluable comments and insights.

References:

Episodes:
Doctor Who
> "Planet of the Daleks" (1973)
> "The Last Christmas" (2014)

Authors:
Alston, William. (1976). "Two Types of Foundationalism." *The Journal of Philosophy* 73.7: 165-185.

Bronowski, Jacob. (1978). *The Origins of Knowledge and Imagination*. New Haven and London: University Press.

Fantl, Jeremy. (2003). "Modest Infinitism." *Canadian Journal of Philosophy* 33.4: 537-562.

Gettier, Edmund L. (1963). "Is Justified True Belief Knowledge?" *Analysis* 23: 121-123.

Hardwig, John. (1991). "The Role of Trust in Knowledge." *The Journal of Philosophy* 88.12: 693-708.

Holley, David M. (2010). Meaning and Mystery: What it Means to Believe in God. Malden, MA: Wiley-Blackwell.

Klein, Peter D. (1998). "Foundationalism and the Infinite Regress of Reason." *Philosophy and Phenomenological Research* 58.4: 919-925.

_____. (1999). "Human Knowledge and the Infinite Regress of Reasons." *Philosophical Perspectives* 13, Supplement of *Epistemology* 33: 297-325.

_____. (2003). "When Infinite Regresses are Not Vicious." *Philosophy and Phenomenological Research* 66.3: 718-729.

Klein, P. (2007). "Human Knowledge and the Infinite Progress of Reasoning." *Philosophical Studies* 134: 1-17.

Lehrer, Keith. (2000). "Externalism and Epistemology Naturalized." *Epistemology: An Anthology*. Edited by Ernest Sosa and Jaegwon Kim with the assistance of Matthew McGrath. Malden, MA, Oxford, and Australia: Blackwell Publishing.

McCain, Kevin. (2016). *The Nature of Scientific Knowledge: An Explanatory Approach*. Switzerland: Springer International Publishing.

Plato, Anastaplo, G., & Berns, L. (2004). Plato's *Meno*. Newburyport, MA: Focus Pub./R. Pullins Co.

_____. Burnyeat, Myles, M. J. Levett. (1990). *The Theaetetus of Plato*. Indianapolis: Hackett.

Zagzebski, Linda T. (1996). *Virtues of the Mind: An Inquiry into the Nature of Virtue and the Ethical Foundations of Knowledge (Cambridge Studies in Philosophy)*. Cambridge: Cambridge University Press.

7

ON ENDINGS, AND OTHER DEPRESSING THINGS

> I always rip out the last page of a book... Then it doesn't have to end. I hate endings!
>
> —Eleventh Doctor ("The Angels Take Manhattan," 2012)
>
> Never let him see the damage. And never ever let him see you age. He doesn't like endings.
>
> —River Song ("The Angels Take Manhattan," 2012)

Do you hate endings, and if so, why? Endings are some of the most natural things in the universe. Sunsets end, meals end, songs end, our lives end, and yes, even the longest running sci-fi show must end one day—it's already happened once! Endings can be scary and sad, but should we hate them? According to the quotes above, the Doctor hates endings, so much so that he never reads the ends of books. I'm afraid, however, that his claim of hating endings is an example of Rule #1: the Doctor lies. The Doctor, and more generally, *Doctor Who* does NOT hate endings. One of the show's main themes is that things end. The Doctor's life comes to an end every few years, and the time he shares with his companions usually only lasts a year or so. Sure, these events are sad, but they are not to be hated. *Doctor Who* primarily promotes the acceptance and embracing of endings. Its main lesson is that if we engage endings like we do life, they enrich our existence, provide closure, and give us the opportunity to mature and grow. For some readers, those who've suffered great loss, you're probably thinking "ridiculous," but I hope from exploring *Doctor Who*'s lessons on endings you'll begin to see their value.

The TARDIS Rotation Method

Let's begin by examining an existential explanation for why we might not like endings. Think about your favorite Doctor. When you heard he was leaving the show, did you find yourself celebrating, or did you find yourself panicking—who are they going to get, you can't replace him, will it be the same show? This is natural. We become accustomed to things, and when we find something we like, we don't want it to end. When the Ninth Doctor regenerated into the Tenth, I said, "I just don't know if I'm going to like this new guy." Of course, this "new guy" was David Tennant, and by the middle of his first season, he'd blown me away too. This is how life and endings typically work. Something ends, something new is introduced, and we can't imagine liking this new thing. We're happy and comfortable with the old, but after a period of time we come to love the new thing just as much, if not more, than the old. We must learn to recognize that things change and we must learn to become comfortable with this change.

Yet, change remains scary. The Danish philosopher Søren Kierkegaard (1813-1855) discusses such a fear with what he calls the aesthetic life. The aesthetic life is a life concerned only with beauty and its resulting pleasure. As Kierkegaard notes, beauty and pleasure are among some of the most short-lived events in our lives. Most of life is working, paying bills, and if you're lucky, having a companion in which to share your life. Because of this, the aesthetic life is filled with the dread that pleasure will come to an end. To avoid pleasure's end, Kierkegaard suggests that the aesthetic life must use what he calls "the rotation method," where you constantly change and replace pleasures in the hope of keeping things fresh and new.

Imagine you love *Doctor Who*, but you only have one episode—no books, magazines, or any sort of other *Doctor Who* paraphernalia. How long will it take before you get tired of your one episode? If it's hard to imagine such a thing, imagine eating the same food every day. Eventually, you're going to get tired of it. The excitement and enjoyment of the thing, whether it's food or your favorite TV show, begins to wear off. To avoid this happening, you need to watch other episodes, or other TV shows, or try eating different things. If you don't use the rotation method, then you'll quickly grow to despise the thing you once loved. Kierkegaard warns, however, that even with the rotation method, the life of the aesthetic contains an ever-present threat of boredom and monotony.

In order to avoid such a life, *Doctor Who* suggests we fill our lives with meaning and purpose. It doesn't mean we ignore or avoid pleasurable things in life, but we shouldn't make those things the center of our lives. We must recognize that pleasures are apt to end, and that if the only thing of meaning in our life is pleasure, we've set ourselves up for failure. Instead, we should focus our lives on things that are meaningful and long-lasting. Such things typically carry with them their own set of pleasures. When we're lucky enough to have pleasure in our life, we shouldn't take it for granted. The Doctor teaches that we must learn to recognize and enjoy each moment, realizing that each one only lasts a mere fraction of second, and that we never know what the next moment will bring. Instead of worrying about losing that one precious moment, or worrying about what the future might bring, we must learn to be comfortable in and take advantage of the now. We delight in what is, and ignore what was or what could be. This is a difficult lesson that few master, but the more we take a realistic approach to pleasure, and learn to focus on things that are long-lasting and meaningful, the more likely we are to flourish. When we take this approach to life, endings have no power over us. Of course, even for those who are successful at this, the fear of death is often the most difficult to overcome.

Life, Death, Afterlife

One of humanity's greatest fears is their mortality. As I note in "Why Time Lords Do Not Live Forever," one of the most common features of religion is that it provides an account of what happens when you die. Some stories of afterlife are more complicated than others, some are pleasant, and some are to be avoided at all costs, but each account addresses a deep-rooted fear humans have about their mortal existence. As a result of this fear, death becomes the enemy. It's the great unknown, and it appears to rob us of this plane of existence, but is death really the enemy?

Philosophy is one of the few areas of life that isn't afraid to talk about death. In Plato's dialogue *Phaedo*, Socrates claims that one of philosophy's greatest virtues is that it prepares us for death. What Socrates means is that philosophy makes us approach death in a critical and logical way, separating what reason tells us from what our fearful imagination says. When we rationally consider death, Socrates argues that there's nothing to fear. In Plato's *Apology*, upon receiving his death sentence, Socrates argues that death is either something or nothing. If it's something, then it should resemble in some way the process of change we currently experience, except that it will be populated by people who died before us. So, when we die we get to hang out with everyone who preceded us in death. If it's nothing, then death is liking taking an eternal nap, which unless you think getting a little extra shut-eye is bad, you shouldn't fear it. Based on these two possibilities, which are both positive, death is nothing to fear.

In the previously mentioned *Phaedo*, Plato uses the voice of Socrates to offer a slightly different account of death. In the dialogue, Socrates builds off an argument made in the *Meno* (that the soul exists prior to our life on Earth) to argue that the soul is immortal. With knowledge of the soul's immortality, we should direct our lives towards The Good (what later theologians describe as God), using reason and wisdom to focus on ultimate reality, while avoiding the distractions and ignorance of earthly physical pleasures.

It's always difficult talking about death with the Doctor, since he doesn't die. Yet, *Doctor Who* does provide an account of the afterlife, though like Plato's two dialogues, they differ slightly. As I argue in "Why Time Lords Do Not Live Forever," the Classic Series suggests that there's no subjective afterlife, in the sense that when a person dies they continue having new subjective experiences similar to the ones they had while alive. Instead, the Classic Series suggests that at some point subjective life simply comes to an end, and that it's perverse to want to be immortal. Look at what happens to Lord Borusa in "The Five Doctors" (1983). His desire to be immortal leads him to kidnap and kill innocent people, and he's punished by being made immortal, as a living stone figure on Rassilon's tomb. The Master seeks immortality, and it only leads to insanity, destruction, and most often death. "The Three Doctors" (1972-73) provides us with one of the most shocking examples of immortality, Lord Omega. Omega's immortality trapped within the anti-matter universe produced a hatred and resentment that ate away every other part of himself, leaving only his will to destroy.

Instead of a subjective experience, the Classic Series suggests a type of objective immortality (at least for Time Lords), where all of the thoughts and experiences of each Time Lord is perfectly preserved in the Amplified Panatropic Computer Network known as the Matrix. Time Lords, then, have a type of immortality, but it's not a personal immortality. Rather, it's an immortality that allows for their experiences to be perfectly preserved for all future generations.

Similar to the Matrix, the New Series suggests that it's possible to capture the mental experiences of individuals. As seen in "Dark Water" and "Death in Heaven" (2014), Missy uses Time Lord technology to upload the mental data of everyone who dies. However, these two episodes suggest that within the Nethersphere individuals continue to have subjective experiences, similar to what happens to River Song in "Forest of the Dead" (2008).

So, what we end up with is exactly what Socrates suggested. Either death leads to a nothingness similar to the Classic Series Matrix, or it leads to change, as illustrated by the Nethersphere in the New Series. Which one is right? We probably won't ever know until we die, but regardless, as Socrates suggests, neither is to be feared.

Just This Time Everyone... *Dies*

For such a life-affirming show, *Doctor Who* has a lot of death. Of course, as I've just discussed, *Doctor Who* isn't afraid of death. It's a natural end of our human existence. What is more, *Doctor Who* often gives us stories of heroes engaged in life and death struggles, and sometimes these heroes sacrifice their lives in order to save others. Jabe gives her life to save everyone on the space station Platform One ("The End of the World," 2005). Harriet Jones, Prime Minister (yes, we know who you are), saves the universe in "Stolen Earth" (2008), but only by sacrificing her life in order to "call" the Doctor. Finally, Donna Noble sacrifices her life in "Turn Left" (2008), in order to preserve a timeline where the Doctor lives and is able to continue saving the universe.

All of these examples are what Aristotle would call acts of courage. They are examples of people making tough moral decisions in the face of death. Instead of being a coward, or acting foolishly, they risked their lives in the face of danger, and died saving others. For many, there's not much in life nobler than giving your life to save others. Interestingly enough, in his *Nicomachean Ethics*, Aristotle argues that life is one long test of being courageous. Aristotle maintains that we should use our impending death as the basis for acting and making the best of this life. As the Doctor suggests at the conclusion of "The End of the World," instead of spending our time worrying about asteroids, politics, disasters, and death, we should make the best of our life on Earth by living courageously in the face of these facts of human existence. So, for Aristotle, death brings value to life. Without death, the fear is that there would be no motive to act, unless you just really wanted to do something. If we're immortal, then we can waste this life and hope for the best in the next. Death, however, puts this life in perspective, and inspires us to make the best of the time we have on Earth.

If you share Aristotle's outlook on life and death, then death isn't the worst thing that can happen to a person. As John Hardwig discusses in his book *Is There a Duty to Die?*, there are certain things, like unbearable pain and suffering, and causing others to suffer and die, which are worse than death. The New Series seems to support Aristotle and Hardwig. For example, Amy's decision to commit suicide in "Amy's Choice" (2010) illustrates that, for her, the loss of a close loved one is worse than death. The Doctor's willingness to go along with Amy implies that he agrees. Another example occurs in "The Angels Take Manhattan" (2012), when Amy and Rory decide to commit suicide instead of living in a world of continual suffering. In both of these examples, everyone ends up surviving, but not every episode has such "happy" endings. In one of the most shocking examples of a character choosing death over life, in a non-heroic way, is Adelaide Brooke in "The Waters of Mars" (2009). In an attempt to defy the Tenth Doctor's "Time Lord Victorious," Adelaide kills herself. She claims that the Time Lord Victorious is wrong, and that instead of living in such a world, she ends her life. No matter their reasons or the story's outcome, these characters preferred death over continued existence, which suggests that death isn't the worst thing that can happen in this life.

I'm in no way suggesting that *Doctor Who* supports suicide, and I would plead with anyone who's had suicidal thoughts to seek help. But it does support the idea that death isn't the worst thing that can happen to a person. Based on what we've just discussed, death is simply an end that should not be feared. It's not even the worst thing that can happen to us. Instead, death should motivate us to make the best of the life we have, and should teach us that it takes courage to risk our lives in the face of death. As Aristotle and the Doctor suggest, choosing to live our lives is an act of courage that rids death of any power it might have over us.

The End of Birth

Death isn't the only ending *Doctor Who* is interested in exploring. Birth, which is most often celebrated as the beginning of life, can be one of the most devastating ends for some couples. During "Asylum of the Daleks" (2012), viewers discover that Amy and Rory have separated due to their inability to conceive a child. For the Ponds, and for all real-life couples who can't conceive, the inability to produce a child is one of the most devastating ends imaginable.

The ability to bear children is one of the oldest and most natural worries of humans. Generally speaking, humans are biologically driven to reproduce. Historically, a woman's ability to bear children has often been closely associated with her value in society, and her inability sometimes seen as a curse. Spend some time reading ancient texts, like the Hebrew Scriptures, and you'll see how important it was that a woman be able to bear children. Of course, contemporary studies have shown that it's most often the man who is at fault, but the stigma still exists in some areas and families that a barren woman is "less-than" one who's able to produce children.

The Doctor doesn't deal directly with these social biases, but we know he's against anything that arbitrarily devalues any sort of life, which is what happens when we associate a person's value to some arbitrary ability—even if that ability is the ability to bear children. Nevertheless, *Doctor Who* does show the devastating effect of not being able to conceive children. In addition to "Asylum of the Daleks," the episode "The Girl Who Waited" (2011) gives viewers a glimpse into the anger and resentment that can develop as a result of wanting and waiting. Just as the years waiting on Rory and the Doctor made Amy bitter, waiting on having a child can not only tear couples apart but it can cause individuals to question their own purpose and existence. For those who've never experienced such anguish, it sounds strange and it's hard to empathize, but *Doctor Who* provides viewers with a glimpse inside the pain of couples and individuals who've suffered this devastating end.

What lesson does *Doctor Who* have for us who can't have children? As always, it tells us not to give up. It tells us to refocuses our energies, to reexamine our priorities, and to develop new strategies for how to "have children." It teaches that you can get involved in mentoring, teaching, fostering, adopting, and being an advocate for children. It doesn't teach us that there will never be any heart-wrenching pain when you see families doing things you'll never be able to do, but it teaches us that we can use that pain to grow and mature. We can help others, especially the millions of children that so desperately need and want someone to unconditionally love them, who need someone to take them on their journey through space and time. In other words, it teaches us to reinterpret one end into a new beginning, focused on what we can do, not on what we can't.

The Doctor's End

> Courage isn't just a matter of not being frightened, you know. It's being afraid and doing what you have to do anyway.
>
> —Third Doctor ("Planet of the Daleks," 1973)

Too often with endings we focus on what's lost, but *Doctor Who* teaches viewers to focus on what can be, on using endings to make ourselves better persons. Nothing illustrates this principle as nicely as the Doctor's death and regeneration. In "The Tenth Planet" (1966) the Doctor's "body wears thin" saving the universe. In other words, he worked himself to death helping others. The Cybermen were simply the final straw. Did he quit? No. He became more energetic, and as a result of his increasing activity saving the universe, he winds up getting punished by the Time Lords for "meddling" ("The War Games," 1969). Did he stop meddling, or just give up trying to save the universe? No. He meddled even more.

The Third Doctor's tenure came to an end when his greed for knowledge ended in a massive dose of radiation ("Planet of the Spiders," 1974). He learned his lesson, and sat out on a new adventure as a "scarfy" artist and philosopher. His commitment to helping others never ceased, and the Fourth Doctor's end occurs when he falls to his death protecting the universe from the Master ("Logopolis," 1981). This doesn't deter him one bit, for in the very next episode the Fifth Doctor is fighting the Master again ("Castrovalva," 1982). The Doctor might change clothing, his looks, and his character, but as R. Alan Siler notes in "Magnetic North," the Doctor's magnetic north—the direction he always points—is to be good and to help those in need. So, when the Fifth Doctor's end comes, we find him again sacrificing his life for a friend ("Caves of Androzani," 1984).

The Sixth Doctor hits the universe with a little more energy and a lot more color than his predecessors, and his commitment to save the universe is just as brilliant. He's again put on trial for "meddling" ("The Trial of a Time Lord," 1986), and by the time it's all said and done, it's up to the Seventh Doctor to fight the good fight. The Seventh Doctor's end comes as a result of gang violence and human error (*Doctor Who: TV Movie*), but he returns as passionate and debonair as ever. Like Socrates drinking his hemlock, the Eighth Doctor's end is a self-administered action designed to create a "Doctor" capable of ending the Time War ("The Night of the Doctor," 2013). The War Doctor wears thin after preventing the genocide of the Time Lords ("The Day of the Doctor"). The Ninth ends by saving his friend Rose ("The Parting of the Ways," 2005). The Tenth ends by saving his friend Wilfred ("The End of Time," 2009-2010). The Eleventh ends saving the town of Christmas ("The

Time of the Doctor," 2013). We don't know what will happen when the Twelfth Doctor's tenure comes to an end, but based on everything we've seen for the past fifty years, the Doctor will stay true to his "magnetic north," carry on learning from endings, and doing what he's always done: take care of the universe.

Each ending brings us an opportunity for something new. It shows us what's important and it helps refocus our lives. Take, for instance, the Eleventh Doctor's final monologue in "The Day of the Doctor" (2013):

> Clara sometimes asks me if I dream. "Of course I dream," I tell her, "Everybody dreams." "But what do you dream about?" she'll ask. "The same thing everybody dreams about," I tell her, "I dream about where I'm going." She always laughs at that. "But you're not going anywhere, you're just wandering about." That's not true. Not anymore. I have a new destination. My journey is the same as yours the same as anyone's. It's taken me so many years, so many lifetimes, but at last, I know where I'm going, where I've always been going. Home...the long way round.

If the Doctor's correct, then we're all heading "home." Home isn't necessarily that building where you keep your stuff, with all those rooms for sleeping. No, home is where you feel most comfortable. It's an accomplishment of hard work and dedication. Home is the safest place for you to dream and reflect upon what's important. So, where is your "home"? For the Doctor, it's a return to helping those in need, and sure he's still looking for Gallifrey, but more importantly, he's looking for meaning and peace. And like any good flâneur, he's going to take the long way to get there.

One of the most interesting aspects of "The Day of the Doctor" is what appears to be a hint into the Doctor's "home." If the Curator is truly the Fourth Doctor, then we gain insight into the true character of the Doctor. A curator is a caretaker of important things, things that would otherwise be lost or destroyed. With the Curator and the Doctor side-by-side, the Doctor's life as "curator" of the universe comes in sharp relief. By understanding them as dual-illustrations of the Doctor's true nature, the dialogue between them takes on a new level of meaning:

> **Eleventh**: I could retire and be the curator of this place.
> **Curator**: You know, I really think you might.
> **Eleventh**: I never forget a face.
> **Curator**: I know you don't, and in years to come you might find yourself revisiting a few...but just the old favorites...eh? You were curious about this painting, I think. I acquired in remarkable circumstances. What do you make of the title?
> **Eleventh**: Which title? There's two: "No More" or "Gallifrey Falls."
> **Curator**: No, that's where everybody is wrong. It's all one title, "Gallifrey Falls, No More." Now, what would you think that means, eh?
> **Eleventh**: If Gallifrey didn't fall, it worked, it's still out there.
> **Curator**: I'm only a humble curator, I'm sure I wouldn't know.
> **Eleventh**: Then, where is it?
> **Curator**: Where is it, indeed? Lost. Shh! Perhaps, things do get lost, you know. Now, you must excuse me, you have a lot to do.
> **Eleventh**: Do I? Is that what I'm supposed to do? Go looking for Gallifrey?
> **Curator**: It's entirely up to you. Your choice, eh? I can only tell you what I would do, if I were you. If I were you...oh, if I were you. Or, perhaps I was you. Or, perhaps you are me—congratulations! Or, perhaps it doesn't matter either way. Who Knows? [Touching his hand to his nose] Who knows?

The Curator's last few cryptic words suggest they're the same, and that the heart and soul of the Doctor—his "home"—will always be to take care of the universe, no matter what endings try to get in his way.

Are we courageous enough to learn this lesson and to do the same? If we are, then we must learn to embrace endings. It doesn't mean we have to enjoy them, and that we can't grieve endings, but we must view them in proper perspective. We must see that every ending creates the possibility for a new beginning, and if we're prepared and courageous (no matter how scared we are), we can take advantage of each ending life throws our way to make all time and space a better place.

References:

Episodes:
Doctor Who
> "The Tenth Planet" (1966)
> "The War Games" (1969)
> "Planet of the Daleks" (1973)
> "The Planet of Spiders" (1974)
> "Logopolis" (1981)
> "Castrovalva" (1982)
> "The Five Doctors" (1983)
> "Caves of Androzani" (1984)
> "The Trial of a Time Lord" (1986)
> "Survival" (1989)
> *Doctor Who: TV Movie* (1996)
> "The Parting of the Ways" (2005)
> "The End of Time" (2009-2010)
> "The Night of the Doctor" (2013)
> "The Day of the Doctor" (2013)
> "The Time of the Doctor" (2013)

Authors:

Aristotle. (2001). *The Basic Works of Aristotle*. Edited by Richard McKeon. Introduction by C.D.C Reeve. New York: The Modern Library; first published by Random House, 1941.

Hardwig, John, with Nat Hentoff, Daniel Callahan, Cohn and Joanne Lynn, and Larry R. Church. (2000). *Is There a Duty to Die: And Other Essays in Bioethics*. New York: Routledge.

Kierkegaard, Søren. (1973). *A Kierkegaard Anthology*, edited by Robert Bretall. Princeton: Princeton University Press.

Lewis, Courtland. "Why Time Lords Do Not Live Forever: Immortality in

Doctor Who." Time and Relative Dimensions in Space: Religion and Doctor Who. Edited by Andrew Crome and James McGrath. Darton, Longman and Todd, 2013.

Plato. (1999). *The Collected Dialogues of Plato, Including the Letters*, 17th edition. Edited by Edith Hamilton and Huntington Cairns. New Jersey: Princeton University Press; first published, 1961.

Siler, R. Alan. (2015). *More Doctor Who and Philosophy: Regeneration Time*, edited by Courtland Lewis and Paula Smithka. Chicago and La Salle: Open Court.

8

DOCTOR WHO AS RELIGION

"I'm the Doctor, and I save people."
—Twelfth Doctor ("Flatline," 2014)

There are a lot of different religions that range from the very private and simple to the very public and complex. There's a lot of ignorance and misinformation about different religions, some is the result of propaganda spewed from biased media and corrupt pulpits, while some the result of personal laziness and racism. Add to all of this the multitude of ways to view, understand, and define what counts as 'religion' vs. 'cult', and we shouldn't be surprised that religion is one of the most disagreeable topics a person can discuss. Whether a person is religious or not, religion strikes a nerve in most people, one which can tear people apart faster than a black hole sucking in an "impossible planet." Still, even with the contentious nature of religious discussions, it shouldn't be avoided. Religion has the power to provide our lives with meaning and purpose, and though it can inspire us to be mean and evil, it can also inspire us to do great and wonderful things. When it inspires the latter, it mirrors the Doctor's mission to get viewers to see a better way of life and to live it. But is *Doctor Who* religion?

Doctor Who's relation to and status as religion has become a hot topic. PBS Idea Chanel's video "Is Doctor Who a Religion?" provides several reasons for why *Doctor Who* is a religion. It begins by citing Clifford Geertz's claim that religion is a system of symbols that organizes people around a general order of existence (a cosmology), which answers questions about the meaning and purpose of life. The video continues by suggesting that, like all world religions, *Doctor Who* provides a cosmology of symbols that organizes its fans in such a way that fills their lives with meaning and motivates them to follow the teachings and lessons of the god-like Doctor. Similarly, Gladstone's "How *Doctor Who* Became My Religion" claims *Doctor Who* is religion because it provides the feelings of a relationship with God, a savior from evil, who is a fallible friend who needs us. It's a religious experience that emotionally moves and teaches Gladstone about the nature of the universe. There have even been several books on the religious and mythical themes within *Doctor Who*, the two most notable being Andrew Crome and James F. McGrath's *Time and Relative Dimensions in Faith: Religion and Doctor Who* and Anthony Burdge, Jessica Burke, and Kristine Larsen's *The Mythological Dimensions of Doctor Who*.

On a very basic level, religion is a set of human beliefs and practices directed towards the worship of the divine (or the unseen). So, studying religion allows us to learn about ourselves, others, and how we understand the entire universe. In fact, religion is such a deep part of human existence, that many instances of art, history, literature, music, eating habits, violent conflicts, and moral values can't be fully understood without understanding the religious symbols referenced. For instance, *Moby Dick* is just a boring old book detailing the life of a fisherman, if you have no knowledge of the religious symbolism seen throughout Melville's masterpiece. With an understanding of these symbols, it comes alive with meaning. Even within *Doctor Who*, the Doctor's angelic ascension in "Voyage of the Damned" (2007) takes on a whole new dimension if you're familiar with the story of Jesus of Nazareth's ascension in the Christian scriptures. You don't need a religious background to understand the episode, but it adds extra meaning if you do.

It's this meaning that enriches the lives of so many religious people. The great theologian Paul Tillich described religion as "the ultimate concern." John Hick, another profound theologian, described religion as deemphasizing the self through the seeking of salvation via the divine. Along these same lines, William James refers to religion as belief in an unseen order that challenges us to move towards the supreme good. Finally, in *Hearing the Call*, Nicholas Wolterstorff eloquently describes the "simplicity, sobriety, and measure" of having a relationship with a God who actually loves and suffers with us.

I've shown that *Doctor Who* creates similar experiences in viewers, though I've framed the discussion in terms of a philosophical way of life. Is *Doctor Who* more than just a way of life? Is it a religion? Or is it something entirely different, something that shares features of both philosophy and religion?

What Religion Is (and Isn't)

The first thing to do is discuss the difference between religion and theology, since they describe two very different things. Religion is about human practice and ritual. It comes from the Latin *religiō*, and is used to describe human conscientiousness and piety towards a deity. Theology, on the other hand, is the study of God—*theos* being Greek for 'God'. So, when we talk of religion the focus is on how humans are reverent towards the divine being(s) they worship, and has nothing to do with the nature of the deity in itself. All good critical thinkers strive to be clear about the question they want to answer, and realizing that we're only interested in the human practice of worship, not in the nature of what they're worshiping—at least not directly—is key to ensuring we actually answer the question "Is *Doctor Who* Religion?" and not some other question, like "Is the Doctor God?"

Another important thing to keep in mind is that there are many different ways to be religious. This is seen in the fact that there are many different world religions that span the globe (First peoples, African, Judaism, Christianity, Islam, Sikhism, Zoroastrianism, Hinduism, Buddhism, Jainism, Taoism, Confucianism, and among others, Shintoism), and there are several religious traditions unique to a particular geographical areas. Within each of these religions is a set of different religious practices. For instance, within Christianity, Catholics and Protestants worship differently. Within Protestant denominations, Baptists and Pentecostals worship different. Even particular denominations, like Baptists, have vastly different worship styles. In addition to these historically recognized religions, worldviews like capitalism, communism, being republican or democrat, and yes, even television shows like *Doctor Who* are sometimes considered religions.

It's this last group that we must examine if we're to determine whether or not *Doctor Who* should be understood as religion. Simply saying something is a religion doesn't make it one. *Doctor Who* might resemble religion, because of the nature of the show and its fan-base, but in order to be labeled "religion," it must meet certain criteria. In order to know the criteria required to be labeled religion, we must examine the nature and history of religious practices and the term 'religion' itself.

Scholars who study comparative religions have attempted to provide a list of criteria of what all religions share. I don't have the space to cover them all, but I'll briefly discuss two lists. First, Lewis Hopfe provides the following six characteristics of a world religion:

1. Features a relationship to the unseen
2. Includes stories of the unseen
3. Contains a set of organized rituals
4. Provides an account of afterlife
5. Provides a code of conduct
6. Generates large followings

Doctor Who seems to share most of these characteristics. It generates a large following. As this book argues, it provides a general code of conduct, both within the show and within the fan community. It has organized rituals at conventions around the globe, and as I argue in "Why Time Lords Do Not Live Forever," it provides an account of afterlife.

The two characteristics it might not share with other world religions is that it does not seem to feature a relationship with the unseen, nor does it include stories of the unseen. In a broad sense, we could argue that the show's mythos, both in terms of the characters but also of the creators, advocates, detractors, and other contributors to the show, provide a relationship and stories to an unseen, but these are different than typical religious beliefs. Take, for instance, religious scripture. Most world religions have scripture that informs and enriches the religion. Followers often base their religious beliefs and practices on how their scripture describes the unseen. The scripture becomes a conduit in which adherents can properly worship. Unless you believe in the divine inspiration of *Doctor Who*, then this doesn't seem to be the focus of the show. *Doctor Who*'s mythos more closely resembles the historical disagreement over the authority, history, and translation of scripture. This sort of disagreement involves an unseen (the unknown history of the scripture), but the unseen is not the divine; it's the historical quirks of producing a meaningful set of documents.

There is, however, another type of relationship with the unseen provided by *Doctor Who*, and that is the relationship it creates between individuals and the fictional character the Doctor. A fictional character is by definition unseen, since it's ultimately a figment in the imagination of an author until being brought to life by an actor or illustrator. This claim has argumentative traction, but it's qualitatively different from the *real* unseen that Hopfe and other religious persons claim to be a characteristic of world religions. A religious person might claim they can't know for certain that their divine exists, that they can't know every aspect of their religious mythos, but their worship is at the very least based on the faith-claim that the unseen does exist. To worship the Doctor is to worship a fictional unseen, and to worship a fiction runs the risk of stripping the religious act of meaning. One might reply that the Doctor represents concepts of goodness and justice, and that it's these concepts that we worship. If that's the case, then the unseen are the concepts, and not the Doctor; which suggests the Doctor would be the means by which one communes with the unseen, but is not the unseen. I feel like I'm beginning to talk in circles, which is more common among philosophers than you might expect, so it might be time to move the discussion forward. Nevertheless, if the above is correct, then *Doctor Who* fails to meet all of Hopfe's characteristics; but maybe Hopfe's characteristics are too strict.

Ninian Smart, a renowned scholar of comparative religion, provides a different set of characteristics:

1. Contains rituals for participation
2. Provides a mythological explanation of the universe
3. Contains doctrinal rules for proper worship
4. Provides ethical standards
5. Creates a social component for human interaction
6. Is experiential, in the sense that participants can in some way experience the divine

Doctor Who fares better with Smart's list. As already mentioned, it contains rituals, provides a mythos, has internal and external doctrinal rules, provides ethical standards, and creates a social framework of interaction. Does it allow participants to experience the divine? Well, yes and no. As seen in the discussion of Hopfe, it's difficult to say that a fictional character is an actual god, so we wouldn't want to say that *Doctor Who* allows us to experience god-as-the-Doctor. However, if the Doctor (or more generally, *Doctor Who*) presents ultimate truths that allow viewers to experience and better-understand the character and nature of the divine, then yes, it allows viewers to experience the divine indirectly through these truths.

We, then, have a conceptual grounding for the claim that *Doctor Who* is religion. However, the truth of this grounding will depend upon whether we focus on the need for an actual unseen, transcendently divine being, like Hopfe, or on the actions and structures that organize the life of religious persons, like Smart. To shed light on which approach might be closer to the truth, let's shift gears and examine the term 'religion' itself.

The Rise of Religion

By some, the word 'religion' is considered as sacred as the god that is the focus of the religion, but as Paul Griffith shows, 'religion' is best understood as a recent invention. In contemporary times we use 'religion' to describe all sorts of different belief-systems, but it didn't arise as signifying separate and distinct worldviews until the Reformation, in the 16th century. It was during this time that Protestantism split from Roman Catholicism. By 1648's Peace at Westphalia, which brought the Thirty-year's War to an end, regions gained the right to determine whether they would be Catholic or Protestant, and so they began categorizing sects of Christianity

(Lutheranism, Zwinglianism, Calvinism, etc.) as 'religions'. As Eastern spiritual beliefs migrated to the West, those that gained official recognition were called religions, whereas belief systems (including some Christian sects) that failed to be called religions were labeled "cults."

As Charles Taylor thoroughly discusses in *A Secular Age*, it's around the time of the Reformation that religion began moving back into the private sphere of life, while secular ideologies (politics and national identity) began defining the public sphere of life. In the centuries following the Reformation, secular interests like art, music, science, economics, politics, and many other pursuits slowly began to dominate public life, and these slowly became what many people considered the focus of life and meaning. Just look at the things on which we spend our time and money: skyscraper banks, big-budget movies, and fan conventions. To fully understand the complex historical development of secularism would take several volumes, but for my purpose, we need look no further than the rise of Humanism. Since *Doctor Who* doesn't provide us with an actual living deity, and since it seems to present divine truths in terms of human achievement, Humanism is the best candidate for grounding *Doctor Who* as religion.

Doctor Who as Humanist Religion

If *Doctor Who* is a religion, then maybe it's a type of Humanist religion. 'Humanism' has multiple meanings and implications, but at its heart is the praise of human ability, achievement, and potential. First developed in the Renaissance, its roots can be traced back to earlier philosophies that praise the human ability to reason and self-govern. The Renaissance was fertile ground for Humanism because people had the time, money, knowledge, technology, and leisure to develop human talents and skills beyond what had previously been seen—think Leonardo Da Vinci! Humanism gained momentum during the Enlightenment, when people began looking for answers that didn't require the mystical and the divine. So, no matter the form of Humanism to which you ascribe, the focus will always be human intellect and ability. Everything else detracts from the near-infinite potential of humans.

Because of its emphasis on human ability, Humanism is often

considered in opposition to theism, spiritualism, and the supernatural, since such things shift the focus away from humans. There are, however, many types of Humanism. Pragmatic Humanists often believe in God, but reject mysticism in favor of empirical scientific enquiry. They're often deists, because they believe that God created the universe but isn't actively involved in its workings. A second category, secular Humanists can be atheist or deist, but either way, questions of God are of little importance. Science and understanding the secular world are often their main concerns. Spiritual Humanists are often a type of existential theist or spiritualist that focus on the existential fears and anxieties of humanity.

Finally, though not exhaustively, Marxists, existentialists, and naturalists maintain that only what can be seen (or understood through some sort of scientific process) can be known, and instead of asking questions about the unseen, we should focus on the material conditions of humanity and how our decisions make such conditions better or worse. William James, who tried to create a bridge between Humanist empirical inquiry and religious rationalism described Humanism as "the doctrine that to an unascertainable extent our truths are man-made products too. Human motives sharpen all our questions, human satisfactions lurk in all our answers, all our formulas have a human twist...The world is what we make it." Another helpful quote about Humanism comes from Paul Kurtz, who suggests Humanism is summed up with the belief that "it's possible to lead a good life and contribute significantly to human welfare and social justice without a belief in theistic religion or benefit of clergy."

Is *Doctor Who* a Humanist religion? It definitely celebrates humans. One of the best examples of the celebration of humans is seen in "Impossible Planet" (2006), when the Tenth Doctor says, "Stand still, I'm going to hug you...Humans, absolutely brilliant and completely mad." Other examples are seen in the Eleventh Doctor's command to "be extraordinary" ("Cold Blood," 2010) and Rose's speech at the end of "The Parting of the Ways" (2005). Of course, it also warns humans of their potential to do evil. It shows us what happens when we fill our lives with hatred (Daleks), or when we try to erase our humanity (Cybermen). Some of the lessons show how greed can ruin your life (Adam in "The Long Game" (2005) and IDW *Prisoners of Time* comic series). One of the most chilling examples of "ordinary" human evil appears in "Midnight" (2008), where the ignorance and stupidity of humans culminates in a competition of who's willing to throw people to their death. Finally, as I argued in "Philosophy, *Fantastic*!", *Doctor Who* challenges us to see beyond our narrow shortsightedness of greed, hatred, and willful ignorance, and instead, strive for knowledge and wisdom.

I could list many more examples, but it wouldn't support the claim that *Doctor Who* is a Humanist religion. *Doctor Who* definitely presents a Humanist philosophy, but it seems to lack the mystical unseen nature so often associated with religion. Fans derive inspiration and are emotionally moved by the show, some are even obsessed, but it's unclear that they actually *worship* the show—at least not in the way one would worship a transcendent deity. If there were proofs outside of *Doctor Who* (say, from NASA) suggesting the existence of Time Lords, then we might have grounds for claiming that *Doctor Who* is a religion, but without the unseen, it appears to be missing the vital component that would make it a religion.

Such a conclusion is in no way negative. Humanism doesn't have an unseen portion, and Humanists aren't upset. In fact, trying to create a "Humanist religion" by incorporating the worship of something unseen seems to diminish both concepts. It becomes a Humanist position that shifts focus away from human reason and ability to the worship of a non-human authority figure. There are worse things that can happen, but in terms of Humanism, things that detract from human ability go against its basic principles.

Maybe the best approach is to view *Doctor Who* as a middle road between Humanism and religion. Alexander Bertland suggests something similar in "*Doctor Who* as Philosopher and Myth Maker." As Bertland shows, it's easy to think the Doctor always supports Humanist and scientific values, but in fact, he often strikes a balance between both science and myth. What this suggests is that the universe is worse off when we only have either science or myth; and when both work in concert, they enrich our lives, help us recognize truth, and provide meaning. Think of the scene in "Gridlock" (2007), when what seems to be a fairly secular society communes through the singing of old hymns, or in "Snakedance" (1983), when the Doctor encounters a secular and cynical society that must rely on spiritualism in order to combat the Mara.

So, when we watch *Doctor Who* it teaches important Humanist lessons like the importance of living authentic engaged lives, seeking truth, helping those in need, being fantastic, being extraordinary, and having no regrets, no tears, no anxieties. While at the same time, it fosters a sense that there might be a realm of the unexplained and unseen worthy of worship—that an authentic religious life can be one of the greatest experiences of our human existence.

Benediction

Have I answered the question: "Is Doctor Who Religion?" No. But as the Doctor shows us, the fun part isn't in answering the question, it's in the process we undergo in trying to answer it. Just as Socrates is famous for leaving questions unanswered for readers to ponder, sometimes even providing contradictory answers (see *Meno*), *Doctor Who* delights in having viewers think and engage in answering questions themselves. Philosophy and life are interactive enterprises that each one of us must choose to participate in, and when we do, we enrich both our own life and the world around us.

It might surprise some readers, but I don't see *Doctor Who* as a religion, though I see how others might. I tend to side with Hopfe, emphasizing the need for the "unseen" in religion. Without some sort of unseen, 'religion' seems to be a hollow term that equates with every other ideology. For me, *Doctor Who* is most properly understood as a philosophy—a way of life that promotes a mixture of Humanist and religious values. This doesn't diminish *Doctor Who* in anyway. It just shows us that it's different and special.

Maybe the reason so many people want to call *Doctor Who* a religion is because so much of contemporary life lacks meaning, while *Doctor Who* provides an abundance of meaning. In this sense *Doctor Who* is akin to what Rudolf Otto calls "the holy." Have you ever revisited a place you loved to visit as a kid? Do you get a special feeling when you return to that place, as though it is holy or sacred? That's the sort of feeling Otto tries to describe with "the holy." He describes such a feeling as something so good it's beyond good, as though there's a dependence between you and the object that grips and stirs your very being.

Otto's sense of "the holy" is what I experience with *Doctor Who*. It's a powerful feeling that is the closest thing I've ever felt to religious transcendence outside of a religious setting. Yet, the realization that it is fiction—though I wish it weren't—prevents me from describing it as religious. I think 'sacred' and 'holy' are probably good descriptors for the show, and I think others often confuse these feelings with the feelings associated with religion. It's not a bad thing to confuse the two, but as good critical thinkers, we should always try to use the right terms.

Nevertheless, if people want to call it religion, I celebrate their excitement. So much of popular culture, and life itself, is void of meaning and purpose. One of the great things about *Doctor Who* is that it's full of meaning and it provides lessons that show viewers their life has purpose. As long as you're not hurting others, and you're striving to be a better person and create a better world, then all I have to say to you is… Allons-y!!!!!

References:

Episodes:
Doctor Who
    "Snakedance" (1983)
    "The Long Game" (2005)
    "The Parting of the Ways" (2005)
    "Impossible Planet" (2006)
    "Gridlock" (2007)
    "Midnight" (2008)
    "Cold Blood" (2010)

Authors:
Bertland, Alexander. (2010). "Doctor Who as Philosopher and Myth Maker." In *Doctor Who and Philosophy: Bigger on the Inside*, edited by Courtland Lewis and Paula Smithka. Chicago and La Salle, IL: Open Court Press.

Burdge, Anthony, Jessica Burke, and Kristine Larsen. (2010). *The Mythological Dimensions of Doctor Who*. Crawfordville, FL: Kitsune Books.

Crome, Andrew and James F. McGrath. (2013). *Time and Relative Dimensions in Faith: Religion and Doctor Who*. London: Darton Longman & Todd.

Gladstone. (Accessed July 2015). "How *Doctor Who* Became My Religion." http://www.cracked.com/blog/how-dr.-who-became-my-religion/.

Griffiths, Paul. (2003). "Religion." In *Philosophy of Religion: An Anthology*, edited by Charles Taliaferro and Paul Griffiths. Malden: MA: Blackwell Publishing.

Hick, John. (2010). *Evil and the God of Love*. New York: Palgrave Macmillan; originally published in 1966.

Hopfe, Lewis M. and Mark R. Woodward. (2011). *Religions of the World*, 12 edition. New York: Pearson.

James, William. (1984). *William James: The Essential Writings*, edited by Bruce W. Wilshire. Albany: State University of New York Press.

Kurtz, Paul. (1983). *In Defense of Secular Humanism*. New York: Prometheus Books.

Lewis, Courtland. (2010). "Philosophy, *Fantastic!*" In *Doctor Who and Philosophy: Bigger on the Inside*, edited by Courtland Lewis and Paula Smithka. Chicago and La Salle, IL: Open Court Press.

_____. (2013). "Why Time Lords Do Not Live Forever: Immortality in *Doctor Who*." In *Time and Relative Dimensions in Faith: Religion and Doctor Who*, edited by Andrew Crome and James F. McGrath. London: Darton Longman & Todd.

Melville, Herman. (1992). *Moby Dick*, or *The Whale*. New York: Modern Library; originally published in 1851.

PBS Idea Channel. (Accessed July 2015). "Is *Doctor Who* a Religion?" https://www.youtube.com/watch?v=3Csjr8bXvPw.

Otto, Rudolf. (1923). *The Idea of the Holy*, translated by John Harvey. Oxford: Oxford University Press.

_____. (2003). "The Numinous." In *Philosophy of Religion: An Anthology*, edited by Charles Taliaferro and Paul Griffiths. Malden: MA: Blackwell Publishing.

Plato. (1999). *The Collected Dialogues of Plato, Including the Letters*, 17th edition. Edited by Edith Hamilton and Huntington Cairns. New Jersey: Princeton University Press; first published, 1961.

Taylor, Charles. (2007). *A Secular Age*. Cambridge: Belknap Press of

Harvard University Press.

Smart, Ninian. (2008). "The Dimension of Religion. In *Exploring Philosophy Religion: An Introductory Anthology*, edited by Stephen Cahn. Oxford: Oxford University Press.

Tillich, Paul. (1957). *Dynamics of Faith*. New York: Harper & Row.

Tipton, Scott and David Tipton. (2013). *Prisoners of Time*. San Diego: IDW.

Wilken, Robert Louis. (2003). *The Christians as the Romans Saw Them*. New Haven: CT: Yale University Press.

Wolterstorff, Nicholas. (2011). *Hearing the Call: Liturgy, Justice, Church, and World*, edited by Nicholas Wolterstorff, Mark R. Gornik, and Gregory Thompson. Grand Rapid, MI: William B. Eerdmans Publishing.

EPILOGUE

> One day, I shall come back. Yes, I shall come back. Until then, there must be no regrets, no tears, no anxieties. Just go forward in all your beliefs, and prove to me I am not mistaken in mine.
>
> —First Doctor ("Dalek Invasion of Earth," 1964)

This journey is coming to an end, but you're just beginning a new one. If what I've said is true, then I began this book in 1983 during my first experience watching *Doctor Who* with my grandfather, and though I've had my ups and downs over the past thirty years, it's been fantastic. Life, and the joys that are contained within every experience, are often taken for granted. The desire to travel back in time and use what you know now to make better decisions when you were younger is the fundamental realization that life can go better or worse depending on the choices we make. The Doctor shows us that it's pointless trying to go back into our own time-stream and change the past. Look at what happens to Rose in "Father's Day" (2005). Trying to change the past is futile. Even in "The Day of the Doctor" (2013) he doesn't really change his past. If he'd erased the past, then he'd have no memory of the events between the Ninth Doctor and the Eleventh (2005-2013). At the end of "The Day of the Doctor" he would've been a completely different person, unrecognizable by viewers. Instead of erasing the past, he created a new timeline: one in which he still has the memories of the children he killed, yet one in which he also prevented those deaths. (I know it's confusing. See Massimo Pigliucci's "Could the Doctor Have Avoided Trenzalore?" in *More Doctor Who and Philosophy*.) With this lesson in mind the best we can hope for is that we take advantage of every last millisecond of the life we have *now*.

Wisdom is NOT about memorizing facts, being rich, having influence, or winning arguments. Wisdom is about truth. And though we fill our lives with many "truths" (truths of mathematics, who won the Super bowl, what's the Doctor's real name), the "truth" of life can't be known, can't be found in formulas, and can't be achieved simply by doing what others tell you to do. The "truth" of life must be lived, and it requires a certain amount of trust in yourself and others around you. It should, then, be no surprise that both *truth* and *trust* come from the same root word *trēowe*. No matter what fills your life with meaning, explains your existence, or motivates you to act, they all require trust—trust that you're acting correctly and trust that it'll result in living a good life. The more we discover about the nature of reality through science, the more we should be in awe of what we don't know. The more we're inspired through religion, "the holy," and shows like *Doctor Who*, the more we should thirst for science and knowledge. Every question and discovery should generate new sets of questions, and the more we learn the less we should understand.

Do you really care about truth or do you just want to prove yourself right? The former is the focus of *Doctor Who*, while the latter is the life of the fool. The easiest lie in the world is the one you tell yourself to justify your desire to be right. Do you want to live a meaningful life? If you do, then you'd better focus on truth, or you'll find yourself so lost, you'll learn nothing. Are you scared of being wrong? If you are, good. You should be scared. As the Third Doctor says, courage is "being afraid and doing what you have to do anyway" ("Planet of the Daleks," 1973). We're all wrong from time to time, but it's only through being wrong and growing from our mistakes that we mature and understand truth.

I hope something in the previous pages will help you along your journey, and if we're both lucky, I hope our paths cross one day. Until then, may your TARDIS always take you where you need to go, and may you find peace in all you do. Farewell, fond companion…

References:
Episodes:
Doctor Who
"Dalek Invasion of Earth" (1964)
"Planet of the Daleks" (1973)
"Father's Day" (2005)
"The Day of the Doctor" (2013)

Authors:
Pigliucci, Massimo. (2015). "Could the Doctor Have Avoided Trenzalore?" In *More Doctor Who and Philosophy: Regeneration Time*, edited by Courtland Lewis and Paula Smithka. Chicago and La Salle: Open Court Press.

INDEX

A.

"A Christmas Carol," 22, 38
"A Town Called Mercy," 49, 63, 64
Ace (Dorothy Gale McShane), 32
Adelaide Brooke, 86
Aesthetic, 22, 82
"The Age of Steel," 48
"The Almost People," 13
Amy Pond (Amelia Pond), 3, 11, 50, 63
"Amy's Choice," 86
"An Unearthly Child," 39, 58, 59
"The Angels Take Manhattan," 81, 86
Aristotle, 10, 23, 85, 86
Asimov, Isaac, 57
"Asylum of the Daleks," 86-87
"Attack of the Cybermen," 61
autonomy, 22
"The Aztecs," 13

B.

Baker, Colin (Sixth Doctor), 85
Baker, Tom (Fourth Doctor), 4, 22, 59
Barbara Wright, 39, 58, 59
"Battlefield," 32
Baxendale, Trevor, 45
"The Beast Below," 22, 48
beauty, 9, 18, 26, 82
black hole, 92
"Blink," 8

"The Brain of Morbius," 14

C.

Capaldi, Peter (Twelfth Doctor), 54, 88, 92
Carrionites, 14, 37
"Castrovalva," 88
causal, 35, 37
"The Caves of Androzani," 24, 27, 88
"City of Death," 18
"The Claws of Axos," 51
"Cold Blood," 98
"The Crimson Horror," 55
Cryons, 61
Cyber Controller, 47
Cyberman/Cybermen, 3, 8, 14, 29, 42, 45-48, 51, 61, 68, 69, 87, 98

D.

Da Vinci, Leonardo, 97
Daleks, 4, 20, 22, 29, 42-45, 48-52, 59, 61, 63, 70, 71, 98
"The Daleks," 59
"Dalek Invasion of Earth," 103
"Dark Water," 51, 84
Davison, Peter (Fifth Doctor), 11, 34, 88
Davros, 22, 49, 61
"The Day of the Doctor," 59, 63, 64, 88, 89, 103

"Death in Heaven," 51, 84
Deception, 3
Descartes, René, 72
determinism, 35-37
"Dinosaurs on a Spaceship," 24, 48, 63, 64
Doctor Who and Philosophy: Bigger on the Inside, preface, 25, 45, 47
Doctor Who: TV Movie, 88
"The Doctor's Wife," 18
Donna Noble, 27, 85
"Dragonfire," 61

E.
Eccleston, Christopher (Ninth Doctor), 60, 82, 103
"The Edge of Destruction," 16
egoism, 46, 47
eirenéism, 26
"The End of the World,"13, 85
"The End of Time," 88
"Enemy of the World," 48
"Evil of the Daleks," 50
"Evolution of the Daleks," 49, 50
Existentialist, 19, 98

F.
"The Family of Blood," 28
"Father's Day," 103
feminist ethics of care, 25
Fendahl, 162, 265
"The Fires of Pompeii," 48
"The Five Doctors," 29, 84
"Flatline," 54, 62
"Flesh and Stone," 11
"Forest of the Dead," 85
forgiveness, 5, 60, 62-65
foundationalism, 72-75, 78, 79
French, Peter A., 56

"Frontios," 34

G.
Gaiman, Neil, 18
Gallifrey, preface, 21, 29, 68, 89, 90
Gandhi, Arun, 65
Genocide, 13, 44, 88
"Genesis of the Daleks," 4, 20, 22, 49, 59
"The Girl Who Waited," 87
Gladstone, 93
Glover, Jonathan, 42, 49
Green, Bonnie and Chris Willmott, 45
"The Green Death," 13, 22
"Gridlock," 99

H.
Hartnell, William (First Doctor), 16, 103
hatred, 5, 43, 48, 64, 84, 98
"Hide," 43
Hobbes, Thomas, 283-88
Holmes, Sherlock, 23, 103, 105
Homosexuality, 163, 220
Hopfe, Lewis M, 94-96, 93
"Horror of Fang Rock," 8
Hostess, the, 39, 41
human nature, 5, 9
"Human Nature," 28
Hume, David, 47, 72
Hurt, John (War Doctor), 88

I.
Ice Warriors, 14

"Into the Dalek," 43, 61
"Invasion of the Dinosaurs," 285
"Invasion of Time," 202
"The Invisible Enemy," 22

J.
James, William, 93, 98
Jesus (of Nazareth), 93
Jo Grant, 142, 165, 200-02, 204
"Journey's End," 22
Judoon, 25, 58, 74

K.
K-9, 22
Kahler-Jex, 64
Kant, Immanuel, 21
"The Keys of Marinus," 5
Kiss, Elizabeth, 25
Krinoid, 161-62
Kuhn, Thomas S, 9
Kurtz, Paul, 98

L.
"Last Christmas," 72
"The Last of the Time Lords," 22
Lewis, Courtland, 83, 84, 91, 95, 101
Loch Ness Monster, 41
"The Long Game," 32, 98
Lumic, John, 48

M.
"Marco Polo," 13
Martha Jones, 35
Master, the, 10-12, 14, 22, 51, 63, 84, 88
The Matrix, 36, 84, 85
Mavic Chen, 7
McCoy, Sylvester (Seventh Doctor), 32, 88
McGann, Paul (Eighth Doctor), 88
Middleton, Harry, 39
"Midnight," 98
Milgram, Stanley, 43
Mill, John Stuart, 19
Moffat, Steven, xi, 28-30, 46, 59, 69, 76
More Doctor Who and Philosophy: Regeneration Time, 103

N.
Nestene Consciousness, 50
Nietzsche, Friedrich, 51
"The Night of the Doctor," 88
"Night Terrors," 22
"Nightmare in Silver," 18
Nozick, Robert, 21

O.
Otto, Rudolf, 100

P.
"The Pandorica Opens," 84, 240, 264, 268
PBS, preface, 1, 92
"The Parting of the Ways," 7, 27, 88, 98
Pertwee, Jon (Third Doctor), 32, 34, 68, 87, 88, 104
Pigliucci, Massimo, 103
"Planet of the Daleks," 68, 87,

104
"Planted of the Ood," 27
Plato, 10, 70, 83, 84
"The Poison Sky," 42

R.

Rassilon, 84
rationality, 17, 18
Rawls, John, 58
Reeves-Stevens and Judith and Garfield, 33
"The Rebel Flesh," 13
Reliabilism, 73-76, 78
"Resurrection of the Daleks," 49, 61
"Rise of the Cybermen," 48
River Song, 81, 85
"Robots of Death," 22
"The Romans," 13
Rory Williams, 86, 87
Rose Tyler, 7, 8, 29, 88, 98, 103
"Runaway Bride," 28

S.

Sarah Jane Smith, 4, 20
"The Satan Pit," 22
Saturnynian, 49
"School Reunion," 22
Sea Devils, 14
"Shakespeare Code," 35
Silence, the, 14
Silurians, 49, 63
"The Silurians," 13
Singer, Peter, 19
Slitheen, 14, 44, 45
Smith, Matt (Eleventh Doctor), 24, 43, 63, 64, 81, 88, 98
"Snakedance," 99
Socrates, 10-12, 47, 69, 70, 83-85, 88, 99
Solomon, 48, 63, 64
"The Sontaran Strategem," 42
"Spearhead from Space," 50
"Stolen Earth," 85
Star Trek, 33, 36, 39, 40
Syilva, J.J., 25

T.

TARDIS, 8, 22, 33, 36, 38, 58, 59, 69, 70, 73-77, 104
Taylor, Charles, 97
Tennant, David (Tenth Doctor), 67, 82, 86, 98
"The Tenth Planet," 47, 61, 87
Theaetetus, 10
Thomas, Laurence Mordekhai, 43
"The Three Doctors," 84
Tillich, Paul, 93
Time Lord Omega, 84
Time Lords, 21, 22, 27, 34, 36, 59, 65, 83, 84, 88, 91
"The Time of the Doctor," 24, 25, 51, 88
Time War, 21, 63, 64, 88
"The Time Warrior," 32
Trenzalore, 24, 103
"The Trial of a Time Lord," 59, 61, 88
Troughton, Patrick (Second Doctor), 41
"Turn Left," 85

U.

"An Unearthly Child," 39, 58, 59
"The Unquiet Dead," 62
Utilitarianism, 19-23, 46, 58

V.
"The Vampires of Venice," 49, 62
Van Gogh, Vincent, 20
Vashta Nerada, 14, 42
"Victory of the Daleks," 49

W.
"The War Games," 59, 88
"The Waters of Mars," 86
Weeping Angels, 8, 14, 42
Wilfrid Mott (Wilf), 88
Wilken, Robert Louis, 102
Wolterstorff, Nicholas, 26, 61, 93

ABOUT THE AUTHOR

Doctor Courtland Lewis received his Ph.D. in 2012, and became a companion of the Doctor in September 1983. He wrote and co-edited *Doctor Who and Philosophy*, its sequel, *More Doctor Who and Philosophy*, and *Red Rising and Philosophy*. He edited both *Futurama and Philosophy* and *Divergent and Philosophy*. Courtland is Assistant Professor and Program Coordinator of Philosophy and Religious Studies at Owensboro Community and Technical College. He regularly attends conventions in order to spread philosophy's love of wisdom, and has contributed to several popular and academic publications, the most recent being *Time and Relative Dimensions in Faith: Religion and Doctor Who*, *Behind the Sofa* (a collection to aid Alzheimer's research), and *Philosophia*.

CPSIA information can be obtained
at www.ICGtesting.com
Printed in the USA
LVHW110258290819
629371LV00001B/44/P

9 781544 298054